OUTLINE YOUR NOVEL

SCOTT KING

This book is a work of non-fiction.

Outline is Published by Majestic Arts

Cover Photos & Design by Scott King

Edited by Steve Bonario

Manufactured in the United States of America

ISBN: 1984190334

ISBN-13: 978-1984190338

First Edition: February 2018

BOOKS BY SCOTT KING

<u>Elderealm</u>

The Wrath of Dragons

Unchained Shadows <u>coming soon</u>

Queen of Flames <u>coming soon</u>

Tales of Elderealm

<u>Other Books</u>

The Zimmah Chronicles

National Cthulhu Eats Spaghetti Day

The Eye of Hastur

Ameriguns

Resist Them

The 5 Day Novel

Story Pitch

Finish the Script!

DAD! A Documentary Graphic Novel

Holiday Wars

CONTENTS

INTRODUCTION

S'up? I'm Scott King and I have a dark horrible confession to make... for the past week I've been telling people that I have taco soup in my jacket pocket. It's been fun gauging the different reactions to the statement.

I've seen mouths drop open without a sound coming from them. I've seen dozens of raised eyebrows. Tons of people simply respond with "What?" My favorite reaction is when the person's head twitches as if their brain literally can't process what I've said. It's been amazing and I feel it is important that you know this about me so that you know what you are getting into with this book.

Outline Your Novel is not a stuffy academic text. It is written in my own voice, and it's straight to the point with no bull or filler. I'm a former college professor so it's not that I can't write fancy or in an academic style, it's that I don't have anything to prove. I don't need to show off and I think as a reader you will gain more if this book reads as if you and I were hanging out and talking in a coffee shop. That's good, because I like coffee and the best way to get good juicy info from me is to bribe me with coffee.

In *Outline Your Novel,* I plan to teach you how the traditional three act structure makes use of certain beats and how to adapt those beats to make an outline. From there we will cover how to adapt your outline without it feeling formulaic or losing your voice as an author. First and foremost this is a book about craft and the pre-writing process. If you are looking for help with the actual writing process or workflow, check out my book *The 5 Day Novel.*

I love the pre-writing process. It is a magic time when as a creator you have a clear vision of the story you want to tell and you've not had the chance to screw it up with sub-par prose or weak storytelling. The deeper an author gets into writing a novel, the more muddy and less exciting it feels. It's harder to see what is working or to judge if it is good or bad. One of the main benefits of understanding story structure and creating an outline is that it can serve as a guide for those dark times.

Before I wrap up this introduction, I want you to know one of my main teaching philosophies: the only wrong way to write is to not write.

You as a writer need to know that the best way for you to write is whatever way works best for you. So no matter what I tell you in this book or what anyone else tells you, listen to yourself first. What works for one person creatively might not work for the next. So be true to yourself and do your best to take the things I'm trying to teach and adapt them to your own process. I have a lot of ninja craft tips in *Outline Your Novel* and I'm hoping you can get a lot of use out of them.

PART I: STRUCTURE

STRUCTURING & OUTLINING

ONE OF THE main things that separates being an author of a novel from being a writer in other media like film, comics, or theater, is that with novels the author is the sole creator. Novels are not written by a committee with dozens of people contributing to them. At most, they are one or two people who put prose to page to execute a story they feel the need to tell. Being an author means having the freedom to do what you want.

That freedom can be daunting, especially to new writers. When a person can write about anything or make anything happen on the page, how do they pick or decide what to write? That's where understanding narrative structure can help.

Structure is the underlying frame that an author uses to select the order of the events that happen in the story they are trying to tell. The most common type of structure is the three act structure, which we will talk about more in a few chapters. However, things like Orson Scott Card's MICE Quotient or

Joseph Campbell's Monomyth are other ways an author can order the events in their story.

Beyond serving as a guidepost for an author, understanding structure is important for understanding reader expectations. The majority of contemporary novels are told using a three act structure, and every mainstream Hollywood movie also uses it. Viewers and readers have been bombarded by story structure from the time they were little and it has created certain narrative beats that must appear for a story to feel satisfying. By understanding structure, an author can play with reader expectations as well as make sure that the reader's expectation is met.

Whether you intend your novel to have structure or not, it will have one. If it is non-traditional and breaks the reader's expectation in a bad way, readers will declare that it feels off, isn't paced right, or a bunch of other complaints. By understanding structure, and subverting that structure to your own storytelling needs, you gain a tool that makes manipulating reader expectations easier.

Look at *Outline Your Novel*, as an example. This book has a structure. The introduction sets the tone and reader expectations. I use weird humor and explain that this book will be written in my natural speaking voice. From there the book is broken into three parts. Part I is about structure and it is mostly lectures and non-writing assignments that build a foundation, preparing the reader for what will happen in Part II. Part II is about outlining and that is where the meat of the active assignments take place. Part III of this book is about how to use your outline to write a novel, which I'll follow up with a book end that wraps the whole thing up.

There is a method to the structure of this book. I could have started *Outline Your Novel* by jumping right to outlining. That would make sense right? Except that, as I said in the intro, I truly believe there are no hard rules when it comes to writing. I can walk someone through how to do an outline, but if they follow that to the exact letter their outline might feel formulaic. It's much better for a person to understand how structure works and then create an outline. Once they know the general expectations for story structure they can adapt that to fit their voice.

If I cut Part III from the book it would be like giving a kid a fancy toy to play with, but not telling them how to put in the batteries. Plus I really wanted a section to hammer home the point that an author's voice is super important for storytelling. So many writing books focus on formula and equations, forgetting that what makes each and every author special is their unique voice.

Part I of this book lays the ground work. Part II of this book is the meat of what I'm trying to teach, and Part III offers a bit of freedom. If I pull out Part I, then Part II doesn't make sense. If I pull out Part II then Part III is confusing. Each part of the book feeds into the next part, building on what comes before it. The structure of this book allows me to lead readers down a specific path that ends with them feeling empowered enough to outline their own novel. That's the power of structure.

Once you have a full grasp of how structure will work we will shift into outlining. I know "outline" can seem like a bad word. I'm sure some of you reading this now have a bad taste in the back of your mouth and you are cringing at the idea of pre-writing. I respect where you are coming from. All authors have their method. The more books you write the more you will develop your own process that works for you. If you are so far along in knowing who you are as an author and that you hate outlines, then don't outline. If you are still trying to find your voice and figure out who you are then give outlining a chance.

I've interviewed hundreds of authors. I've also attended multiple conventions and conferences where I've chatted with and met both indy- and traditionally- published authors. Although everyone seems to have a different process for how they create a novel, one of the consistencies that almost all authors talk about is being able to reach a flow-state, that in-the-zone moment when the real world fades away and they are able to type without thinking about it. Reaching and staying in that flow-state is an invaluable tool to an author. It's not always easy to get there and the slightest distraction can pull you out of it.

The benefit of using an outline is that it addresses problems that will arise during the writing process. You won't have to stop and think about where a scene is set, what scene is next, or what your character wants in the moment, because all of those things will be spelled out in your outline. Having those answers means that instead of getting distracted, you get to stay focused and in that flow-state.

Outlining and structure are related, but they are not the

same thing. Structure is the basis for how you pick the order of the beats that appear in their story while an outline is a much more fleshed out tool you use when writing their story. Because of how the two are tied together, it is important to understand structure first before jumping into making an outline.

CHARACTER ARCS

IT'S impossible to talk about the three act structure without talking about character arcs, so to make sure everyone has the same ground work, let's go over what a character arc is and look at the main kinds of character arcs.

A character arc is the change a character goes through from the start of your story till the end of your story. For example, if your character starts at point A and by the end of the story they are at point B, or Z, or basically anywhere else but A, that change in them is a character arc.

The most common character arc is to have a protagonist with a flaw and to have them either overcome or fail to overcome that flaw. A flaw can be as big and melodramatic as someone being an alcoholic or something as simple as a character that lies too much. The flaw that a character arc centers around will tie directly to one of the themes of the story you are trying to tell.

For Part I of *Outline Your Novel* I will be referencing a lot of movies. Movies are a great way to teach structure because they live and die by it. Also it's easier for me to say "go watch a two-hour movie" than it is for me to say "Go read this book that will take you a month to read."

Rain Man is a great example of a movie where a character's arc goes through a positive change. In the movie the character Charlie, played by Tom Cruise, is an asshole who cares only about money. The movie opens with him trying to sell fancy imported sport cars, but he's unable to do so because they don't meet the legal emission guidelines. Unable to offload the cars, his business is on the brink of crumbling.

Charlie's father dies and Charlie thinks he's going to get a big pay day, but instead of leaving Charlie money, his father leaves three million dollars to a trust for a secret person. Charlie is pissed. He feels he is owed that money and feels cheated. He uses his slimy sweet-talking skills to figure out where the trust holder is and he goes to confront the trust holder. In doing so, Charlie discovers he has a secret older brother who was diagnosed as being autistic. The three million dollar trust is to pay for his brother's assisted-living needs.

Charlie is furious. He is angry that he has a secret brother. He is angry that his brother gets the money. He snaps. He sort-of kidnaps his brother and plans to take his brother to Los Angeles for a custody battle. His hope is that he can get his brother put into his care, which will give him the control of the money. It's a selfish dick-move and makes his character out to be a horrible character.

As the story progresses, Charlie and his brother make a long road trip from the Midwest to Los Angeles. As Charlie bonds with his brother, scene by scene his anger lessens. When Charlie gets to Los Angeles, the original holder of the three million dollar trust offers Charlie $250,000 to end the custody battle. It's more than enough money to solve Charlie's money problems, but he turns it down. The movie ends with Charlie putting his brother's needs before his own.

Charlie's arc is one where he goes from a selfish asshole only caring about money, to someone who cares about his family. He overcomes his anger issues and he overcomes his greed. The movie is about his character having positive growth.

The basic structure of this kind of character arc is simple…

- Establish a character's flaw.
- Character's flaw causes relationship problems.
- Character's flaw gets in the way of them getting what they want.
- Character is forced to see they have a flaw.
- Character will change or not change (based on the theme you want).

If the novel you are planning is one where you don't want positive growth in a character, then it would be easy to adjust a story like Charlie's to be one where his arc ends in failure. In Act III of the movie when Charlie is offered the $250,000, instead of him turning it down, you could have him take it. This would show that he has not changed and would never change. The theme of the story would shift from a more sentimental one to one where it says humans are assholes and that's just the world we live in.

The next most common type of character arc is one where there is no change. This happens much more rarely in films, but happens all the time in television. It also happens in novels with long-running series like the Dresden Files, Jack Reacher, Stephanie Plum, Pendergast or Dirk Pitt books. When handling a story that is more episodic in nature, it's a bit easier sometimes to have a character who, instead of changing themselves, they inspire change. So maybe one novel in the series has a character arc where the protagonist grows, but the next two have one where instead of the protagonist growing they inspire change in others.

This especially happens in shows like Grey's Anatomy that have an episodic procedural feeling. The main characters grow over the course of a season, but generally in the specific episodes they don't change. They instead inspire change in the sick patients or the families of the sick patients.

Forrest Gump is a great example of a movie with a character that has no growth but inspires others to change. The movie starts off with him sitting on a bench and he shares his life story with a bunch of strangers. From the time he is a boy till the very end of the movie, Forrest Gump is consistently Forrest Gump. However, the character of Lieutenant Dan, portrayed by Gary Sinise, has a full arc.

Lieutenant Dan is first introduced when Forrest Gump is drafted to fight in Vietnam. Lieutenant Dan is half naked with a chiseled chest and is a specimen of confidence and health. He reveals that he has ancestors who died in every American

War since the Revolution and that he sees it as his destiny to die in Vietnam. He isn't suicidal or self destructive. He has a more Zen-like attitude to it and although he has accepted that he will die, he makes it his mission to protect and take care of his men. He will do everything in his power to save as many of them as possible.

A few scenes later, things go wrong. Forrest Gump's squad is attacked and torn up by enemy fire. Many of the men, including Forrest's best friend, are killed. Forrest, because he is Forrest, acts without thinking or processing the risk to himself, and starts carrying his injured squad members out of the jungle to save their lives.

When Forrest finds Lieutenant Dan, Lieutenant Dan is calling in an airstrike. Lieutenant Dan knows it means his own death and he is fine with that. This is what he always expected from life. Forrest, being Forrest, ignores Lieutenant Dan's plea to be left behind, and carries him to safety.

Injured, both Forrest and Lieutenant Dan are sent home from the war. Forrest has a bullet wound in his butt, but Lieutenant Dan ends up with both his legs amputated. Lieutenant Dan's life is drastically altered and he has a horrible downfall, becoming a shadow of the confident Zen-like person we first met.

The story progresses and through a quirk of a weird promise, Lieutenant Dan shows up to serve as Forrest's first mate in a new shrimping business. It's a struggle at first, because Lieutenant Dan is disabled and because the region is overfished. A bad storm comes, wiping out competing fishermen, which fixes the industry, but it also fixes Lieutenant

Dan. With the storm raging, facing death, he comes to terms with what happened to him and he decides he wants to live and can make a life for himself. The final time we see Lieutenant Dan, he has prosthetic legs, a new fiancé, and once more carries himself with that Zen-like attitude and confidence that he had when first introduced.

Lieutenant Dan's arc is very different from the one Charlie goes through in *Rain Man*, and yet they happen in a similar manner. Forrest Gump is a catalyst that causes a change in Lieutenant Dan's life. This breaks the self image that Lieutenant Dan has for himself, creating a flaw. Lieutenant Dan spirals downward, but Forrest forces him to face his flaw. Lieutenant Dan gets to a point where he will either crash and burn or grow, and he decides to grow. He reforms the mental image he has of himself, and overcomes his flaw.

The third kind of character arc is a full downward spiral with no redemption. This happens in all mediums of storytelling, but occurs more often in darker themed genres. The TV show Breaking Bad is a great example. The entire series is about the fall of Walter White. If you are looking toward movies, *Raging Bull* is the classic example.

Raging Bull is the story of boxer Jake LaMotta. It takes place over a twenty year time period and starts in the 1940s with Jake at the beginning of his boxing career. At the time, boxing was one of the most popular sports in the world and everyone talked about it. Jake went on to become the world mid-weight champion. He was a major celebrity. The equivalent of a rock star. He also lost it all and had no one to blame but himself.

Jake dated an underage girl, married her, and abused her. He verbally abused and physically abused his brother. He pushed away everyone that cared about him and even ended up spending time in prison for introducing underage girls to older men. He was scum. He had no redeeming qualities.

The downfall arc is hard to nail right and it's not surprising that Robert De Niro won an Academy Award for best actor for his portrayal of Jake LaMotta. What carries the movie is De Niro's acting. In the film, LaMotta is a powerhouse. He has determination, skill, and the toughness to be a world champion. He could live the dream and have it all. What gets in the way is himself. He is his own antagonist and he deserves every horrible thing that happens to him. It's a dark movie.

When planning ahead for your novel, start thinking about what kind of arc you will want to include. Do you want your character to grow and change, want them to fail to change, want them to inspire change, or do you want them to fall? Whatever your answer, be aware that it will tie directly into the themes of your novel.

ASSIGNMENT:

Watch a movie set in the genre you plan to write and take note of what kind of character arc the protagonist goes through and how that growth, lack of growth, or fall is shown.

THREE ACT STRUCTURE

THE THREE ACT structure is something you've been bombarded with since you were a kid. It's everywhere and you most likely already inherently have an understanding of how it works. Act I is setup. Act II is the messy middle where the meat of your story happens, and Act III is the climax. In writing circles I've often heard the three act structure taught by saying that Act I is characters being chased into a tree, Act II is the tree catching on fire, and Act III is the tree burning down and falling at the same time.

Of all the acts, Act I is the most formulaic. No matter the genre or type of story you are trying to tell there are certain things that simply must happen, and those things generally happen in Act I. Readers must meet the main point-of-view (POV) character. They must meet the supporting cast, learn the rules of the world or society, and then something must happen that will spark a change and kick off the rest of the story.

The easy thing about Act I is that as a writer it can be followed beat by beat without much stress. Because the structure is laid out, it's the best place in a novel for a writer to get a bit more creative and fun. It's the part of the story where you get to push the limits and really define the tone, pacing, and what kind of story you are going to tell.

Act II gets a bad rap and I can understand why. I'd be lying if I said there was never a point in my writing career where I hated Act II. The problem with Act II is that it doesn't fit perfectly into a paradigm, template, or method. That makes it much harder to teach and as a result it gets called lots of bad names.

The secret to understanding Act II is that it's the part of the story where you as the author really get to shine. You get to be yourself and tell the story that's important to you. It is generally the longest part of the story and the place where your voice as a creator shines the most. At its core, Act II is about building up relationships between the characters so that at the end of Act II everything can implode.

Act III isn't as formulaic as Act I, but it's close. Because stories build to a climax, Act III has to be about paying off everything set up in Acts I and II. There will be action or a big flashy argument and then some sort of epilogue to wrap up the theme and any other plot lines.

We will spend a bit of time talking about each act individually, but for now I want you to focus on understanding what causes Act I to transition into Act II and what causes Act II to transition into Act III. To do that, let's examine a summer action movie and a traditional drama.

Wonder Woman, starring Gal Gadot, has clear breaking points for each Act. Act I is her on the island of Themyscira and it ends when she decides to leave the island to kill Ares. Act II ends when she kills a man who she thought was Ares, but it doesn't end the war or save the day.

The film makes the end of Act I and start of Act II visually clear with a setting change. That's normal, but a setting change does not cause the end of Act I. What changed is that the character of Diana gains what I call a Big Want. She decides she wants to kill Ares, and she takes action to make that happen. Act II ends when Diana has made her best effort to achieve her Big Want, but fails. The failure causes a downfall, a moment of crisis that kicks off the start of Act III.

Beyond the plot points of having a want, trying to achieve that want, and failing to achieve it, Diana's character arc mirrors the plot points. In Act I, it is set up that Diana has never left the island of Themyscira. Her view of the world is that it is her duty to protect mankind from Ares. When the other Amazons won't take action to stop World War I, she steps forward, declaring that Ares is behind it. If you had to label her flaw, you could say she is naive and the theme of the movie has a strong coming-of-age feel.

Over the course of Act II, Diana comes to see that humans are monsters. They do horrible things to each other and she keeps telling herself that it is because of Ares. At the end of Act II when she kills the monster who she thought was Ares, the war doesn't end. Her belief system of what humans are fails. She crashes and hits an emotional rock bottom.

In Act III, Diana finds a new hope and understanding of

mankind as well as gets a chance to go after Ares. She develops a new view of humans and that understanding empowers her to defeat Ares. If we were to combine the act breaks with Diana's character arc, the main sections of *Wonder Woman* would look like this:

- Act I - Establish Diana's view of how the world works.
- Act I End - Because of her worldview, Diana leaves Themyscira to end the war.
- Act II - Diana is confronted with reality and forced to question her worldview.
- Act II End - Diana's worldview is shattered and she fails to end the war.
- Act III Start - Diana grows, forming a new understanding of the world.
- Act III - Diana finds Ares and defeats him.

Wonder Woman is a big summer tent-pole movie. Those generally adhere to traditional character arcs and structure a bit more than dramas. So let's break down *The King's Speech*, which won an Academy Award for Best Picture.

The King's Speech opens with "Bertie", the Duke of York, failing to make a speech at a horse race due to a speech impediment. He gets bad advice from a royal doctor who, to the modern audience, appears to be talking out of his butt. As a result, Bertie's wife takes it upon herself to find a doctor that can help her husband. She tracks down Lionel, an expert in the field. Lionel says he will asses Bertie and decide if he will take Bertie on as a client. Bertie agrees to meet Lionel and says he will decide if he will accept treatment from him or not.

The Duke and Lionel met. It's a mess. They butt heads and leave intending to go their separate ways. As Bertie is leaving, Lionel gives him a recording of Bertie himself speaking. Bertie doesn't want to listen because he knows it's crap. Bertie meets with another doctor who is no help. Depressed, Bertie finally listens to the record. He is shocked to discover that in the recording he speaks without stuttering. Bertie and Lionel meet again. They agree to work together to fix Bertie's speech impediment.

The majority of the movie is then about Bertie and Lionel getting to know each other and building a friendship as well as working on the stuttering. Things come to a head when Bertie's father dies and Bertie is set to become the king. He has to attend his coronation and speak there. It comes out then that Lionel is not an actual doctor. He is a failed actor who got into speech therapy while treating wounded veterans. This leads to Lionel and Bertie having a falling out.

They both make amends and decide once more to work together and to continue their friendship. It's perfect timing because war is on the horizon and as a result Bertie has to make a speech announcing war. Together they conquer the problem and Bertie makes the speech without stuttering once.

Over the course of the movie, Bertie has anger issues and a massive problem trusting others. This becomes clear to him when he and Lionel fight, moments before his coronation. His flaws create external conflicts and only by coming to terms with his flaws and growing is he able to deal with his stuttering.

Breaking down the movie it looks something like this…

- Act I - Establish Bertie's anger and frustration over his stuttering.
- Act I End - Bertie agrees to be treated by Lionel.
- Act II - Bertie and Lionel work together on his stuttering and become friends.
- Act II End - Bertie's anger gets the best of him. He lashes out at Lionel ending their friendship.
- Act III Start - Bertie realizes his mistake and grows to overcome his anger.
- Act III - Bertie makes amends and is able to make a speech without stuttering.

Even though *Wonder Woman* and *The King's Speech* are completely different genres the overall structure of how the stories are told is the same. The characters' wants align with the characters' arcs and together they create the standard three act structure.

Act I ends when the POV character develops a Big Want. Act II ends when that character either gets their Big Want and it fails or they fail to get the want. That failure causes the character to hit a rock bottom which launches the story into Act III.

ASSIGNMENT:

Watch a movie in the same genre that you want to write a novel in, and pick out where each act begins and ends.

ACT I

IMAGINE a connect-the-dots style drawing of a horse. The lines between the dots haven't been drawn in, but just from the dots alone, you can probably tell what the image will reveal. Beats are like the story version of those connect-the-dots dots. Beats are moments within a story's structure where specific events, character discoveries, or character realizations must happen.

When we broke down *Wonder Woman* and *The King's Speech*, those bullet pointed sections were beats. The idea is that by figuring out the beats for a story we can build it from the ground up. The basic beats that appear in Act I are:

- Opening Hook
- Meet the Protagonists
- The Status Quo
- Catalyst Moment
- Deal with Catalyst
- The Big Picture

The Opening Hook: The opening is one of the most important parts of a novel. A lot has to happen and if it sucks readers will stop reading and never get to any of the other good stuff. In the opening you want to establish the genre, set up reader expectations, and have some sort of hook that leaves the reader wanting more.

The opening's main goal is to say to the reader "Hey, this is the kind of story that this novel is going to tell." If you are writing an action-oriented novel, the opening should have a bit of action. If you are doing more of a character study, the opening should be slower paced, but really delve and make clear who a specific character is.

The hook in your opening needs to grab the reader's attention and create a spark or mystery that will make the reader continue reading. The hook generally will tie into the genre, but it doesn't have to. For example, if you are writing a romantic comedy, the opening might start with a character being left at the altar. If you are writing a thriller, it might be a character being murdered. If you are writing fantasy, the opening could be some epic battle and hint of what's to come.

Those are over-the-top examples, but they should make the point clear. We will talk a little bit more about teasing and hooking the audience in Part III when we cover mysteries.

Meet the Protagonists: Once the reader knows what kind of story they are going to get, it's time to really introduce your main point-of-view character or characters. Keep in mind that you can have your POV character in the opening so don't think you can't, but unless you are writing more of a character-driven novel, the opening will be more tied to genre than character. Which means after you have established the genre and after you have hooked the reader it will be time to explore and teach your reader who the POV characters are.

At this point you should know what kind of arc your character will have and this sequence should start to establish it. If they have a traditional arc then you will reveal their flaws. If they have a flat or downfall arc, you will start setting up the lack of change or what they will lose when they become self-destructive.

All characters want things. At the end of Act I your POV character will develop a Big Want that will push them through the rest of the story, but early on they should have an Intimate Want. In a traditional character arc the Intimate Want is usually tied to the character's flaw, and by the time Act III rolls around the character discovers that the thing they secretly wanted the whole time was the wrong thing.

The Status Quo: Humans don't act the same all the time. They act differently when interacting with different people or when they are alone. Think of how you might act when around your parents or grandparents. It's most likely not the same way you act when hanging out with your friends. For a reader to understand a character we need to show that the character is layered and has varying facets.

Most people have a work life, a home life, a friend life, and a romantic life. Depending on the genre and type of story you are going to tell, these may slightly differ, but are good go-to examples. The reason they matter is because at the end of Act II your protagonist is going to hit rock bottom. They will fail to get what they want and they will burn bridges with all their relationships. For those bridges to be burned those relationships have to be set up. This is where that happens. This is the part in the story where you start to show the character's life that will burn at the end of Act II.

Catalyst Moment: Your character should exist in a frozen moment of time. When the story starts we get to see what their current life is like, but then something must happen to shake it and kick the story in motion. A catalyst of some sort has to come along. If not, nothing will change for your protagonist.

Of all the beats, this is probably the easiest to nail because without it your story simply won't happen. The catalyst usually comes from an outside force: meeting someone new, a change at work, someone getting sick, a chance encounter, acceptance to somewhere, or something equivalent. The change the catalyst provokes will be so big that your POV character won't be able to ignore it.

Deal with Catalyst: This is a bit of a reprieve where your POV character has to deal with what just happened. Somehow their life got altered and we get to see how this affects the POV character as well as how it impacts the various facets of their lives. Your protagonist has two options. They can accept the change and adapt or they can refuse to accept it.

If they accept the change, the story will continue to the next beat. If they refuse, something will back them into a corner and they will have no option but to accept it.

The Big Picture: Upon embracing the change brought on by the catalyst, your protagonist will develop their Big Want. This new want will drive the rest of the story and be tied to the genre. In an epic fantasy it might be to stop a dark lord. In a romance it might be to win someone's heart. In a thriller it might be to catch a killer. The important thing about the Big Want is that there must be consequences if a character doesn't get it. If they don't achieve their want something bad has to happen. That bad thing is called The Stakes and we will talk about that more in Part II.

ASSIGNMENT:

Take the movie you watched in the last assignment and pick out the beats that occur in Act I.

ACT II

ACT II IS all about the the character's arc and the Big Want that was established at the end of Act I. It's also a free-reign region where, as the author, you are left to your own devices.

Traditionally in films, Act II is split into two halves so that the three act structure becomes a four act structure, but the joy of novels is that you can do whatever you want. Act II is when you get to show your voice and unique view. It's also collapsible and your Act II can be as short or as long as you want.

The easiest way to digest Act II is to think of it as a repeating cycle where your point-of-view character is attempting to achieve their Big Want. If aiming for a shorter Act II then there might only be one or two things preventing your POV character from achieving their Big Want. If you are going for something longer there could be tons of obstacles getting in the way. Expanding or contracting the beats in Act II is the easiest way to adjust the length of the story without making major changes to a story's structure.

The cyclical beats that appear in Act II are:

- New Status Quo
- Big Want Step 1 Attempt
- Big Want Step 1 Fail or Success
- Status Quo Growth
- Status Quo Growth and Big Want Attempt Cycle
- Big Want Final Step
- Rock Bottom

New Status Quo: Having a Big Want will change the POV character's relationships. This will cause a shift in the status quo and this beat is where you show that the relationships are altered from how they first appeared in Act I. Usually, the Big Want will improve relationships and as Act II progresses your POV character will grow closer to the other characters. If creating a story about the downfall of a character, the New Status Quo beats in Act II will be about the weakening of relationships as opposed to strengthening.

Big Want Step 1 Attempt: To achieve their Big Want the POV character will need to do certain things, depending on the genre and story you want. This is the first step in achieving what they need to get the Big Want.

Big Want Step 1 Fail or Success: Your POV character will either fail or succeed at overcoming the thing preventing them from achieving their Big Want. If they succeed, another complication will come up or they will be able to go directly to Big Want Final Step. If they failed, they will have to take a new approach to achieving their Big Want.

Status Quo Growth: With the success or failure, the status quo will once more change. The protagonist will strengthen their relationships and start to become aware of their flaws.

Status Quo Growth & Big Want Attempt Cycle: Depending on the genre and the length of the story you are trying to tell, there will be one or more cycles of Big Want Steps and Status Quo Growths. The POV character will make a Big Want Step 2 Attempt. That attempt will either fail or succeed and the status quo will change as a result. The cycle will then repeat until your POV character is ready to take the final step needed to get their Big Want.

Big Want Final Step: Your POV character is ready to go after their Big Want. Their flaws, which they had appeared to be overcoming, get in the way, and things go bad. The character will either full-out fail to achieve their Big Want or discover the Big Want they had been seeking was the wrong thing and in reality they should have had a different Big Want.

Rock Bottom: The Protagonist has failed to get their Big Want. In addition, the other relationships and life situations they have been building throughout the story will collapse. Any romantic relationships your POV character has will fall apart, their friendships will fail, their career will tank, and their home life will be a mess. Everything that can go bad will go bad.

While your character goes through the cycle, there needs to be a sense of progression. Progression is the secret to Act II. The reader needs to feel like the story is moving forward. Without that progression they will complain about the story meandering and not going anywhere.

The quirky thing about progression is that it's an illusion. It's a construct that the author creates to manipulate the reader. You have to understand that. You have to accept that the whole point is to pull the strings and trick the reader because, to be able to do it right, you have to embrace the concept.

The easiest way way to create progress is to show change. It's why in our Act II cycle we have the Status Quo Growth. Change is seen as progression and that change could be a negative one. Regression in what we are talking about is the same as progression. It's a change. When trying to create a sense of progression, look at changing things up. Do whatever you can to make it seem like there is change… switch the locations, have character arcs move forward, have relationships grow, and have the obstacles standing in the way change. Stagnation is bad and any kind of stagnation will make it feel like there is no progression.

Video games are a great example of intentional design that promotes progression. Most games have levels and beating each one and moving on to the next creates a sense of change. Even open-world games, like *The Witcher 3* or *Fallout*, have areas of the world so that, even if there aren't traditional levels, a character completing quests or missions in a forest may move on to a city.

World of Warcraft, the classic **MMORPG**, is masterful at creating a sense of progression. A new player begins the game in a starting area. The enemies there are super weak, and it's an effort for the player to kill them. As the player completes quests, their character will level up, growing stronger and unlocking new abilities. Eventually they will become too powerful for the starting area and non-playable characters will direct them on a quest that will lead them to a new area. The cycle will repeat and eventually the player will be sent to another area, and then another.

For certain personality types, MMO's are addictive. They have ended marriages and destroyed relationships. The have inspired people to lose their jobs and there have been some people who have literally died because they were so busy playing that they forgot or didn't care about self care. By constantly dangling bits of goodness, MMO's suck gamers into a world and keep them from leaving. The sense of progression is so strong that it's hard for the player to tear themselves away.

In a similar fashion, freemium mobile games, like *Candy Crush*, do exactly the same thing that MMO's do. They create an addictive sense of progression that sucks in players and gets them to spend money. In *Candy Crush*, the player must line up rows of candy. It's a basic puzzle game, but the user interface and system is ingeniously designed.

Candy Crush limits what a player can do in a single day without spending money. Each level is then carefully designed so that the end of the level is always in sight. A player will get super close to finishing, but the daily limit of the app will prevent them from doing so. It dangles the carrot of finishing a level in the same way MMO's dangle the finishing of a quest. It teases the player and manipulates them into spending money.

When creating Act II you need to think like a game designer. You need to tease your readers, offering bits of goodness and a sense of progression so that they never get bored or think that your story is going nowhere.

Below are some of the tricks you can use within your Act II cycle to manipulate your readers.

Character Awareness: If doing a traditional character arc, certain things have to happen. People don't blink and just change on their own. Everyone has a sense of who they are in their own head. For a change to happen, they must first be confronted with the idea that who they are isn't the person they want to be. So for a traditional arc to work, a character's flaw must show itself, cause problems, and force the character to embrace change. They then have to actively try to change.

Characters Level-up: If you are writing genre fiction, where your character literally has magic powers or they are a super hero, you show them progressively getting better at using that power.

If you're writing a non-sci-fi or non-fantasy story you can still do this, but with a skill. Instead of a character getting better at flying or using magic, they get better at skating, or knitting, or whatever skills are needed for your POV character to achieve their Big Want.

Countdown: In screenwriting they often call this a "ticking bomb." It means that at the start of Act II a date or time has been set. Something bad will happen at a specific time and as Act II progresses the countdown to that specific time gets closer. This is used mostly in thrillers, however it can work in any genre. Most Christmas movies use a countdown to create a sense of progression. As Act II ticks by, a calendar will show the days getting closer and closer to Christmas.

The countdown can work for any big event related to the Big Want. Instead of Christmas maybe things are counting down to a big court date for a child custody hearing? Or maybe instead of counting days, the countdown is tied to supplies and the estimated day people in a spaceship or on a lost island will run out of food? A countdown can be used in any genre.

Build Something: Humans understand how things are physically built. It starts small or incomplete, and becomes something big or complete. To create a sense of progression, you can have a character build something. If they are an architect maybe they are designing a house? Act II starts with them struggling to get the design right, but by the end they have it. Or maybe the characters are bakers and they are designing the perfect wedding cake for a competition? The secret to making this work is simply to start from scratch and show the thing being built bit by bit.

Take a Trip: *World of Warcraft* is genius in this. It creates an amazing sense of progression by having characters change settings. If you are trying to tell a story about a journey, give the end point of the journey and show the characters getting closer and closer to that end point. This exact thing was used in *Rain Man* with Charlie and his brother getting closer and closer to Los Angeles.

Growth in Relationships: As people get to know each other, the way they act toward each other changes. If your POV character is treating their supporting cast or co-stars exactly the same way across the whole of your story there will be no sense of change or things moving forward.

Dangle the Mystery Carrot: I mentioned it lightly when talking about opening hooks and will cover it more in Part III of this book, but mysteries are huge way to create a sense of progression, even if you are writing in a different genre. Giving the characters, or even the reader, a bit of mystery and slowly dangling out clues will make the story feel like it is moving forward.

These tricks to create progression are not the only ways to do it, but they should be enough to get you started. Keep in mind, too, that these manipulations aren't exclusive. You can have characters on a road trip and at the same time they are unraveling a mystery or you can have a character getting better at using magic while at the same time everything is counting down to an ultimate wizard competition.

Tackling Act II of a story is daunting, but sticking to the cycle and infusing it with a strong sense of progression will help you from getting lost and making sure that readers don't get bored.

ASSIGNMENT:

Take the movie you watched in the last assignment and pick out the Big Want of the protagonist, then analyze how a sense of progression is created to get the movie into Act III.

ACT III

ACT III IS EVERYTHING a story builds towards. If you lined up all the beats in Act I and Act II then Act III should be easy. It should flow out, paying off the things you've set up without you having to stress or worry about it. In Act III you will resolve your POV character's wants, any kind of arc that you created for them, and any other promises that you made to your readers.

If unsure about what promises you made, go back and look at your opening hook at the start of Act I. If you opened your novel with an action sequence, you need to make sure your third act is chocked full of action. If you were writing a character study, then don't randomly add action. It's those kinds of promises that you need to resolve and breaking them will leave readers feeling unsatisfied.

Consider the themes you've established in your novel. Do they come to an end, leaving questions? It's OK for your theme to ask questions and not give answers, just make sure they close on the points you want them to. For example if you want the underlying theme of your novel to say humans on the whole are good, but your novel ends with the antagonist winning and everyone screwed, that sends a mixed message.

Here are the basic beats that must happen in Act III:

• Epiphany Moment
• Empowered
• Climax
• Temptation Moment
• Epilogue

Epiphany Moment: Your POV character has hit rock bottom. Depending on the arc you are doing, this is the moment where they will grow, fail to grow, or fall. This is them realizing their flawed ways and actively deciding to change or not change things. The epiphany moment is a brutally hard scene to nail right. If you are too over-the-top with it, it will feel cheesy; if it's underdone, then the character arc will feel forced or unearned.

Sometimes an epiphany moment can be small. It might be a character alone, looking at photos, reading letters, or just reflecting upon a lost relationship. Sometimes they are big with a supporting character yelling and ripping your POV character a new butthole. How big or small the epiphany moment is will depend on your voice, the story you are trying to tell, and how important the theme of your story is.

If your story is more of a downfall like in *Raging Bull*, instead of learning from their mistakes and growing, the POV character will embrace the falsehoods they believe, which will destroy them. In *Raging Bull*, Jake LaMotta pushes away his wife and his brother. Instead of learning and growing to be a better man, he blames them. He refuses to take any responsibility for what has happened to him. It is the audience who then has an epiphany moment, realizing that Jake LaMotta is a horrible man who will never change.

Empowered: Once the epiphany moment happens your POV character will fix the relationships and the facets of their lives that they destroyed when hitting rock bottom.

The relationships they fix are those not tied directly to their Big Want. For example, if your protagonist's Big Want was something work related, the relationships they will be fixing here will be with their friends, family, and in their love life. The strength they get from those fixed relationships will empower them so they can make one final attempt to get their Big Want.

Climax: This is the big hurrah and everything your story has been moving towards. It's your POV character having one last chance to achieve their Big Want. Conflict is key for the climax and the stakes are huge. If your POV character does not succeed they will lose everything.

Temptation Moment: The temptation moment really only works in a traditional character arc. If you are not doing one of those you can skip it. In the temptation moment the character is offered an easy way out, a chance to fall victim to their flaw.

This was very clear in Act III of *Rain Man* when the trust holder offered Charlie $250,000 to walk away. That money is what Charlie wanted the whole movie, but he rejects it. He rejects it so the audience can see that he has grown and changed. He is no longer a man who cares about the money. He simply wants what is best for his brother.

In this moment the protagonists will be tempted one final time to give in to their flaw. If you are writing a positive character arc, they will overcome it; if you are writing a negative one, they will give in.

Your POV character will get their Big Want or they will not get it. Not getting it doesn't mean they failed or that your story has a sad ending. Your character may have decided that the thing they were chasing the whole movie was meaningless and by not getting it, they have grown and changed.

Epilogue: The ending will often bookend the start of your story, but it doesn't have to. In the epilogue, the storyline of the supporting cast and any subplots will be wrapped up, and the final scenes usually tie back to the theme of your story. Whatever overt or subtle message that you want to give readers, it will happen here.

ASSIGNMENT:

Take the movie you watched in the last assignment and pick out the beats that occur in Act III.

BEAT SHEET

LET'S put all the beats we have been talking about to the test and use them to break down *Moana*! If you've not seen the movie, I suggest watching it first while trying to pick out the beats yourself, and then coming back here to see the breakdown.

Moana - **Hook:** Maui a mystical shape shifter steals the heart of Te Fiti, a powerful stone that holds the power of creation. Maui is attacked by Te Ka and loses his magical fish hook and the heart of Te Fiti in the ocean.

Moana - **Meet the Protagonists:** We meet a young Moana who goes out of her way to protect a baby sea turtle from birds that want to eat it. The Ocean (actual personification of the ocean) witnesses this and tries to give young Moana the heart of Te Fiti.

Moana - **The Status Quo:** Moana is a teenager now, set to be the next chief. She is growing into a great leader, but the island is suffering. Crops going bad, fishing spots drying up, and she wants to leave the island to find more resources. She also wants to leave because she feels the "call" of the ocean.

Moana - **Catalyst Moment:** Moana tries to leave the island and fails. Her vessel is wrecked. She is ready to give up her idea of leaving and submit to just being a leader.

Moana - **Deal with Catalyst:** Moana confides in her grandmother. Her grandmother reveals a secret cave. Inside are ocean-faring ships and Moana learns her people used to be travelers with wayfinders that sailed from island to island.

Moana - **The Big Picture:** Moana's grandmother dies. Before she does, she gives Moana the heart of Te Fiti and tells Moana that if she wants to save her people she must find Maui, give him the heart, and get him to return the heart to Te Fiti.

Moana - **New Status Quo:** Moana and her pet chicken are sailing to find Maui.

Moana - **Big Want Step 1 Attempt:** Moana tries to sail across the ocean to find Maui, but she has no idea how to find her way or how to properly sail the ship.

Moana - **Big Want Step 1 Fail or Success:** Moana fails at sailing. She gets caught in a storm, but The Ocean steps in and makes sure that Moana gets shipwrecked on the island where Maui is trapped.

Moana - **Status Quo Growth:** Moana finds Maui. She has to convince him to take the heart and restore it to Te Fiti.

Moana - **Big Want Step 1 Attempt:** Moana is direct and tries to use words and reason to convince Maui to take the heart.

Moana - **Big Want Step 1 Fail or Success:** Maui refuses to take the heart. He steals Moana's ship and ditches her. Only through her physical skill and determination is Moana able to catch up to Maui.

Moana - **Status Quo Growth:** The Ocean steps in. It forces Maui to work with Moana. They are then attacked by evil coconuts that steal the heart.

Moana - **Big Want Step 1 Attempt:** Maui and Moana need to get the heart back and escape.

Moana - **Big Want Step 1 Fail or Success:** Moana uses her skill to get the heart and Maui uses his sailing skills to help them escape.

Moana - **Status Quo Growth:** Sailing again, Moana is finally able to convince Maui to restore the heart by saying he will be a hero. Maui says they will, but first they must get back his magic fish hook. Maui also agrees to start teaching Moana how to be a wayfinder.

Moana - **Big Want Step 1 Attempt:** Maui and Moana go to the Realm of Monsters to get the magic fish hook.

Moana - **Big Want Step 1 Fail or Success:** Working together, Maui and Moana get the magic fish hook.

Moana - **Status Quo Growth:** Maui and Moana head to Te Fiti. On the way Moana continues to improve her sailing skills and Maui learns how to use his magic fish hook again.

Moana - **Big Want Final Step:** Moana and Maui try to restore the heart but the fire demon, Te Ka, stops them!

Moana - **Rock Bottom:** Maui's hook is cracked by Te Ka. He gives up the idea of restoring the heart and leaves Moana. Moana, feeling broken and a failure, realizes she will not save her people and gives the heart of Te Fiti back to The Ocean.

Moana - **Epiphany Moment:** Grandmother's spirit talks some sense into Moana. Moana now understands she was never supposed to get Maui and force him to restore the heart. She realizes that she is the one who must to do it.

Moana - **Empowered:** With her new skill of sailing and wayfinding, as well as with the confidence of how to be a leader, Moana sails to try to restore the heart one more time.

Moana - **Climax:** Moana faces off against Te Ka. Maui returns, sacrificing his magic fish hook, and allows Moana to restore the heart.

Moana - **Temptation Moment:** Moana learns that Te Fiti is gone. On the verge of giving up again, she uses her newfound understanding of herself and pieces together that Te Ka is Te Fiti. Moana gives Te Ka the heart and she is healed, becoming Te Fiti again.

Moana - **Epilogue:** Maui is gifted with a new fish hook and then Moana returns home. Once there she shares the knowledge of sailing and leads her people to become voyagers who sail the ocean again.

Moana's character arc through the movie is like this:

• Moana hears the call of the ocean. She wants to sail.

• Moana is torn between being a leader for her people and her desire to sail the ocean. She can't seem to choose between the two.

• Moana sails to restore the heart and lives out her dream of sailing and exploring. She does it in the name of saving her people, but at the same time feels guilt.

• Moana fails to restore the heart, but realizes that her desire to sail and being a leader aren't exclusive. She can be who she is and find balance in her life.

• With a better understanding of who she is and how to balance that with being a leader, Moana uses that knowledge and is able to turn Te Ka back into Te Fiti.

Structurally, *Moana*'s ACT II is a bit short. That makes sense when you consider that it is a classic animated Disney movie. Those traditionally have a shorter running time. Yet even being a shorter film, it still managed to hit all the beats and it did so by truncating its Act II. By having less Big Want Attempt Cycles, it let the filmmakers shorten the movie without losing anything important.

If you are still having trouble identifying beats, watch a mainstream movie in the genre you plan to write your novel in and try to pick out all of its beats. This list below should make referencing the beats easier. Also, keep in mind that not every movie will match perfectly, but the more studio-driven and tent-pole-like movies should be darn close.

Hook: The opening sequence to the story where the author establishes the genre, sets the tone, and starts setting up reader expectations so that the reader will know what kind of story the author is telling. This sequence should include a hook, some sort of mystery, to make the reader want to know more.

Meet the Protagonist: A series of scenes where the reader gets to meet the protagonist of a story. It is important that in these scenes the reader learns what the protagonist's intimate wants are and see why that character currently can't achieve that want. If the character has a traditional flaw or flaws they are revealed here. If the main themes of your story were not introduced in the Hook, they start to be revealed here.

The Status Quo: After meeting the protagonist, the reader needs to learn the life situations of that character. At the end of Act II the protagonist's lives will blow up and this is the first look at what those lives are like.

Catalyst Moment: The life situations of the protagonist must change and that change happens in the catalyst moment. An outside force, another character, or the protagonist's flaws must cause something to happen that spurs change.

Protagonist is forced to deal with change: The protagonist can embrace the change introduced in the catalyst moment or they can resist it. If they resist it, things will go bad, and they will be forced to accept it.

The Big Picture: Upon embracing the change, the protagonist will see the world and their situation differently. In additional to their intimate want they will develop a Big Want. The Big Want is the thing they are trying to achieve throughout the rest of the story.

New Status Quo: Now that the protagonist has a Big Want things have changed and they will find a new status quo in their life and their relationships.

Big Want Step 1 Attempt: To achieve their Big Want the protagonist will need to do certain things, depending on the genre and story you want. This is the first step in achieving what they need to get the Big Want.

Big Want Step 1 Fail or Success: If the protagonist succeeds in their Step 1 Attempt, then they still discover another complication that will lead to Step 2. If they fail Step 1 they will have to take a new approach that will lead to Step 2 or the Big Want Final Step.

Status Quo Growth: The protagonist will strengthen and build their relationships and life situations. There is clear growth and the hint that everything will turn out fine.

Status Quo Growth & Big Want Attempt Cycle: Depending on the genre and the length of the story you are trying to tell, there will be one or more cycles of Big Want Steps and Status Quo Growths. In each cycle it's important that the protagonist's relationships constantly grow and that they constantly get closer to achieving their Big Want.

Big Want Final Step: The protagonist is ready to go after their Big Want. The protagonist's flaw, that has been revealing itself every now and then, will bubble forth and will force cause them to fail at getting their Big Want.

Rock Bottom: The protagonist has failed at their Big Want. In addition, the other relationships and life situations they have been building throughout the story will collapse.

Epiphany Moment: The protagonist finally faces their flaw. This is the moment where they either change or embrace not changing.

Empowered: The protagonist makes amends and rebuilds their relationships. With the strengths gained from those, and the strength from overcoming or giving in to their flaw, they gear up and get ready to make one final attempt to achieve their Big Want.

Climax: The protagonist faces off against whatever has been preventing them from getting their Big Want.

Temptation Moment: In this moment the protagonist will be tempted one final time to give in to their flaw or to deny it for good and prove they have changed. Either way they will also achieve or not achieve their Big Want as a result of this moment.

Epilogue: A book end that wraps up the theme of your story and gives closure to the relationship and life situations of your protagonist.

WRATH OF DRAGONS

I LOVE the classroom environment when teaching how to write. The best part is that when there is a large group of creators where everyone is sharing their work, an individual learns not just when hearing feedback about what they've written, but also when they hear feedback about what others have written.

It's impossible to create that kind of environment in a book. The best I can offer is to do the assignments that I am teaching so that you can see the choices I make, where I mess up, and how I later fix those mistakes.

In conjunction with *Outline Your Novel* I will be structuring and outlining my fantasy novel *Wrath of Dragons*. The first few drafts of *Outline Your Novel* resulted in what has become Part II of this book. I did the assignments and used them to write *Wrath of Dragons*. It wasn't until the Fall of 2017 that I decided *Outline Your Novel* needed Parts I and III. It's not that I felt Part

II was bad, but I felt there needed to be more of a foundation before it and some guidance after it.

In college, I wrote a screenplay called *Dragon Lotus*. It was meh. Not bad. Not good. Just meh. It's been a world that I've wanted to come back to, but I've sat on it for more than ten years feeling my own skill levels weren't where they needed to be yet. That changed two years ago when I did a full rewrite of Dragon Lotus from the ground up and it became *Wrath of Dragons*. The only thing I've really carried over from the original version of the story is the Big Want and voices of the three main POV characters.

Not everyone who reads *Outline Your Novel* will be a fantasy writer and that's fine. The methods that will follow are geared to be used for all genres. You also don't need to read *Wrath of Dragons* before moving on to Part II of this book. However, if you are a fantasy reader, I highly recommend going to read *Wrath of Dragons* first. It's one of the best books I've written and it's better to enjoy it and then come back to see how I structured and outlined it.

In Part II we will be getting our hands gritty. There are a lot of assignments. They might seem random and not related, but they will build on each other, eventually coalescing into an outline, so don't skip them.

PART II: OUTLINING

WHY THIS STORY?

WHAT DO you as an author want for yourself and how you define success? Do you want to write books only for the money? Are you doing it for the purity of art? Are you somewhere in the middle?

I have enough books out that I can make a living telling the stories I want to tell and I write the books that I do because I can't not write. When I don't write I get itchy.

The second half of 2017 was a hectic year for me. In August we had a two-week family vacation with my wife's family. Then we got hit by hurricane Harvey. We were lucky and our town was saved by a levee, while homes a mile down the road had five to ten feet of water in them.

I spent the first part of September volunteering and trying to help out those who had been hit by the hurricane. As that calmed down, my wife found out that work was transferring her from a plant outside of Houston to one outside of Pittsburgh. That meant finding a house, buying it, and getting ready for the move. October was all about moving, and trying to spend time with friends before we hit the road. The move happened and it was second week of November before we were settled again.

From August to the start of November, all I wrote was a ten thousand word short story. That's it. It drove me crazy. I was stressed, not about business or marketing, but because there were stories and ideas in my head and they weren't coming out.

I'm all-in on writing for the sake of story telling. I care less about business. With *The 5 Day Novel*, I proved that I could write fast and I know that if I wanted to crank out rapid releases I'm capable of it, but doing so isn't my sweet spot. I write the stories I want to tell. That doesn't make me better than someone who is more of a pulp writer pouring out stories. It just means I have a different business model.

Being story first means that when I choose what to write there is a reason. I love fantasy novels. Although I read every genre out there, second world and epic fantasies are my go-to genres. They are home. They have given me much over the years and I've always wanted to give back.

That's what *Wrath of Dragons* is to me. It's my love letter to the fantasy genre and I want it to be awesome. I want to tell a story that makes the reader cry and laugh. I want to break hearts. I want to impact readers on an emotional level. The things spurring me to write *Wrath of Dragons* are no better or worse than another author saying, "I'm going to write this book to pay the bills." To be an author you need to know why you want to write a novel because the reasons you choose will inform your writing.

ASSIGNMENT:

Decide why you want to write the novel you want to write and decide who your POV characters are.

STORY PITCH

THE FIRST STEP I like students to take when writing a novel is to create a Story Pitch. A regular pitch is a description of your novel that you use to sell to an agent, publisher, or even a potential reader. A Story Pitch is a tool that you as the author can use when pre-writing, writing, and re-writing your novel. I wrote a whole book about how to create and use a Story Pitch, but I'll do my best to teach a streamlined version of how to write one. If you have any trouble understanding, or want a bit more information about character wants, the stakes, creating conflict, and themes, go read it!

At its core, a story is a character who wants something, but an antagonistic force gets in the way of that want, causing conflict. Additional elements that contribute to a story include: the stakes, genre, the author's voice, and theme. By figuring out these core elements and a few minor elements, it will give you an early view of what your novel feels like. That preview will serve as a foundation that will allow you to figure out the act breaks and develop the beats.

To construct a Story Pitch you need to know these elements:

- **POV Character** - The main point-of-view character of your novel. If you have multiple main-POV characters you can write a Story Pitch centered on each of them.
- **POV's Big Want** - This is the big thing your POV character is trying to achieve throughout Act II.
- **Core Conflict** - This is the antagonistic force that is preventing your POV character from getting what they want. This can be a bad guy, but it might not be. It might be societal rules, money issues, forces of natures, or a bunch of other untold things.
- **The Stakes** - This is the bad thing that will happen if your POV character does not achieve their Big Want.
- **The Genre** - This is the genre and sub-genres of the story you are going to write. It's important that the genre of your story is clear from your Story Pitch.
- **Voice** - This is the unique thing that you the author are bringing to the story that separates it from all the other stories that are already out there.
- **Main Theme** - This is the main theme of your

novel. All stories have theme so you are better off to embrace a theme, even if it's a small one, as opposed to ignoring it.

- **POV's Intimate Want** - The want your POV character has at the start of the story.
- **POV's Character Arc** - If they have an arc you need to hint at what that arc is.
- **POV's Internal Conflict** - If they experience any kind of internal conflict from their wants or the choices they have to make.

Using the movie *Groundhog Day* as an example, here are all the elements of story I need to construct a Story Pitch:

- **POV Character** - Phil Connors, a Pittsburgh weather anchor.
- **POV's Big Want** - Wants to leave Punxsutawney, PA.
- **Core Conflict** - He is caught in a time loop.
- **The Stakes** - If he doesn't escape he will be caught for all eternity in an endless time loop.
- **The Genre** - Comedy, Science Fiction, Time Travel.
- **Voice** - Being stuck in a time loop (at the time the movie was written) was not a mainstream well-known trope and has only appeared in a few smaller science-fiction stories. None of those stories were comedies or vehicles for character growth.

- **Main Theme** - Don't be selfish or a jerk.
- **POV's Intimate Want** - Wants bigger better things in life than his rinky dinky job.
- **POV Character's Arc** - Changes from being an arrogant selfish jerk to someone who goes out of his way to sincerely help others.
- **POV's Internal Conflict** - Must cope and deal with the reality that he may never be able to escape from the time loop.

To start building a Story Pitch, plug in the proper story elements into this template:

A character desperately wants a thing, but this other thing is getting in their way. If they fail to get the thing they want then something bad will happen.

When I plug *Groundhog Day* into the template it looks like this:

Phil Connors wants to escape Punxsutawney, PA, but he is caught in a time loop. If he can't figure out how to break the loop, he will spend all of eternity repeating the same day over and over again.

From there, I can start adding in the missing elements. The genre, voice, and internal conflict are already clear so what are really missing are Phil's Intimate Want, his Character Arc, and a hint of the theme. If I add those the Story Pitch shifts to become this:

> Arrogant weatherman Phil Connors is pissed about having to spend another *Groundhog Day* in Punxsutawney, PA. All he wants is for the day to end, but thanks to a cruel quirk of the fates, he is caught in an endless time loop. Forced to face a reality where he might end up spending all of eternity reliving the same day over and over again, Phil has to choose between indulging his reckless behavior or trying to spend the day making a difference.

All the elements of story are included in the above version, but it's now a bit clunky. Smoothing it out, it looks like this…

> Arrogant weatherman Phil Connors is pissed about having to spend another *Groundhog Day* in Punxsutawney, PA. All he wants is for the day to end, but thanks to a cruel quirk of the fates, he is caught in an endless time loop, reliving the day over and over again. Living in a world with no consequences, Phil indulges his most twisted reckless fantasies, but the excitement fades when he realizes there is no escape and he will forever be trapped in a temporal distortion.

If I wanted to rewrite it, I could, but I think that it gets the job done. It's important to remember that a Story Pitch is just a pre-writing tool. No one else but you will ever see it. It doesn't have to be fantastical, perfectly worded, or pretty. It just has to get the job done. A Story Pitch shouldn't be more than a paragraph long. To include everything it will generally take up three sentences, though depending on your voice and writing style it may take more. When done, make sure not only that it includes all the elements, but also that it excites you. You should be able to read it and ask, "Is this the story I want to tell?" and know the answer instantly.

Steps for Writing a Story Pitch:

- List your answers for all the elements of story.
- Plug the core elements into the pitch template.
- Make sure the genre of your story is clear.
- Add the voice element and don't hesitate to add new sentences.
- Make sure the theme of your story is hinted at.
- If the theme is unclear consider tying a character arc, internal conflict, or more intimate wants into the Story Pitch.
- Check for missing elements.
- Rewrite till you are happy with the results.

Writing your first Story Pitch can be a bit overwhelming. If you want a bit more guidance on the elements of story and how to construct one, pick up my book Story Pitch. Also, if you want a worksheet that can help you with creating one, you can snag one here: http://www.scottking.info/blog/story-pitch-worksheet/

ASSIGNMENT:

Write a Story Pitch for your novel.

WRATH OF DRAGONS:

Wrath of Dragons is such a beast of a novel. I have three main point-of-view characters and three minor point-of-view characters. I won't write a Story Pitch for all six, that's a bit excessive, but I should write one for each of my main characters. First I'll walk through constructing a Story Pitch centered around Carter and then I'll share the ones I wrote for Doug and Alex.

CARTER

- **POV Character** - Carter, a magician's apprentice.
- **POV's Big Want** - Wants to stop the dragon attacks.
- **Core Conflict** - The dragons are being mind controlled and Carter does not have the power to stop them.
- **The Stakes** - If he fails to stop the dragons thousands will die.
- **The Genre** - Epic fantasy.
- **Voice** - Carter's story is a bit more fall, and learning from that, than a traditional farm-boy who gets power.
- **Main Theme** - Carter's Story is a coming-of-age story.

- **POV's Intimate Want** - Wants to be a hero.
- **POV Character's Arc** - Grows to realize what he defines as a hero is not what it means to be a hero.
- **POV's Internal Conflict** - Coming to terms with the fact that the way he sees the world is not how it is.

First Pass at Carter's the Story Pitch:

Carter, a magician's apprentice who desperately wants to be a hero, sees his chance when he learns that dragons are ravaging the kingdom. He quickly discovers that even his powers are not enough to free the dragons and if he can't discover another way, thousands will die and the weight of it will sit upon his shoulders.

It's an OK start. Going through it the Core Conflict could be a bit more clear and so could the hints at his arc.

Second Pass at Carter's Story Pitch:

Carter, a magician's apprentice, desperately wants to be a hero and sees his chance to be one when he learns dragons are ravaging the kingdom. He quickly discovers a dark mage is controlling the dragons and even Carter's powers are not enough to stop him. With the weight of thousands of lives hanging in the balance, he must decide what really matters, being a hero or getting credit for being one.

I dig it. I'm going to do one more minor rewrite and then

I'll share the Story Pitches written from Doug and Alex's POVs. Never forget that a Story Pitch is a tool for the author. It doesn't have to be copy edited or written to perfection. It simply has to be enough to give you a solid structure for the story you wish to tell.

CARTER: Carter, a magician's apprentice who often keeps his head too buried in books, desperately wants to be a hero and sees his chance to be one when he learns dragons are ravaging the kingdom. As the real world shocks some sense into him, he discovers his powers are not enough to stop the dragons. With the weight of thousands of lives hanging in the balance, he must find a way to save them and to do so he has to decide what matters more: being a hero or getting credit for being one.

DOUG: Decades after fleeing the dragon clans, Doug's kin return to the world of humans, killing thousands. In retaliation a "powerful mage" (Carter) accidentally turns Doug into a human and all Doug wants is to be a dragon again. Sucked into a world of magic, dark gods, and horrible creatures, Doug has to learn let go of his hermit ways or risk being stuck as a human for forever.

ALEX: Seeing her kingdom burn and her father unwilling to take action, Princess Alexandra Eos takes it upon herself to stop the onslaught of dragons. Upon discovering a dark mage is controlling the beasts, she has to lead a rag tag group of adventures to find a lost magic. Should they not return in time, her father, everyone she loves, and her people will all die.

ASSIGNMENT REMINDER:

Write a Story Pitch for your novel.

READER EXPECTATIONS

Structure is king when it comes to screenwriting. With novels, genre rules. That means when it comes time to doing your actual outline you have a bunch of wiggle room in terms of how you handle the structure. The downside is that you need to be aware of genres and the expectations that those genres have.

A novel is a promise to a reader. An author creates a story, and in the blurb, cover design, and early chapters, they make promises to a reader saying "Hey, this book is this kind of story." Readers get very upset if they go to read a novel and the story is a different kind of story than the one they were expecting.

For example, *Wrath of Dragons* is an epic fantasy novel. Its sub-genres overlap a bit with coming-of-age, action adventure, and dark fantasy. If in the very first chapter of *Wrath of Dragons* I had an intense scene where two characters were making out and talking about love and their future, but then the rest of the novel had no more mushy or romantic stuff, then I would be making a false promise.

The only way to make sure you are making the right promises to your readers is by being well-versed in the genre you are writing. There are too many genres for me to know how all genres work. I primarily read fantasies and thrillers. If a short story, novella, or novel in another genre becomes a big hit, wins a lot of awards, or develops a lot of buzz, I'll read it. I like to be in-the-know with that kind of stuff, but I'm still not well-read enough to be able to write a romance or historical fiction.

The only way to understand reader expectations is to be a reader. I genre hop all the time in the books that I put out, but I've never put out a book in a genre I don't read. It's why I will never write a romance novel. Not because there is something unworthy about the genre. The genre is the highest selling genre and the readers who read them devour the books. If I wanted to make money, cranking out several romance series would be the way to go, but I don't read romance. I wouldn't know what readers would expect and romance readers get very upset with a romance book that breaks the genre rules.

This all falls back into the old cliché of "write what you know." I've never seen a dragon in real life, but I've read fantasy since I was a kid. I have no problem understanding how to write a story with a dragon as one of the main POV characters. Once you understand a genre and know what tropes, elements, and beats you can twist or subvert, you can then twist them to your own needs to satisfy your own voice and style.

For hundreds of years, dragons have been appearing in fiction. There are generally two kinds: dragons that are animal-like monsters with not much intelligence, and dragons that are fully sentient beings on par with, or greater than, humans.

Going into *Wrath of Dragons* I know I want my dragons to be an intelligent race, with their own culture, language, and history. In the first chapter or two I'm going to have a dragon attack and have them appear as beasts. Monsters. Horrible powerful things. Then that sequence will end with the reveal that dragons are more than beasts. It's not a big earth shattering reveal but it is a way for me to play with reader expectations. I get to set it up to make the reader think one thing, and then shortly after I flip it and reveal the actual story I plan to tell.

I can do this because I've read enough fantasy to know that there are two ways dragons are portrayed. I'm also doing it in a more fun way that will put the reader into the same mindset as Carter, the POV character. Like the reader, Carter will think dragons are foul fell beasts, but he will be shocked to discover that there is more to them. If I wasn't a fantasy reader, I wouldn't know about the different kinds of dragons and couldn't toy with reader expectations. Or I might play with it, but instead of manipulating things in a fun way, I could break hard genre rules and anger readers. Treat reader expectations not as a heavy thing, limiting the story you are trying to tell, but as a tool to manipulate the reader.

As an author, you are trying to invoke and make your readers feel things about a world or characters that doesn't actually exist. You want them to laugh, cry, and connect with the things you've pulled out of your imagination. Knowing your genre, so you can play into reader expectations and twist them, is important.

If you don't already know the genre of the novel you plan to write, now is the time to start reading. Read the best sellers. Read the worst sellers. Check out the reviews and keep on digging till you understand what's special about the genre and what things readers are looking for. Pay attention to the story, characters, but also the mechanics of the storytelling. How many POVs does the genre regularly use? What are the typical lengths and common themes that crop up in the genre?

I've read second world fantasy novels since I was a kid. In the past ten years or so I've fallen off reading some of the adult series, mostly reading YA and middle grade instead. So to prepare for writing *Wrath of Dragons* I made sure I dove in and read *The Farseer Trilogy*, *The Name of the Wind*, *Lies of Locke Lamorea*, *The Blade Itself*, *The Fifth Season*, and *Blood Song*. Sometime soon I also plan to try the *Stormlight Archive* and fantasy series from indy authors.

My dive into contemporary written fantasies told me that the majority of them were written in third person and the pacing was fast with lots of action. What surprised me the most was how gritty a lot of them felt. When there was violence it was gory and the authors didn't shy away from torture, sex, or adult themes.

Although I know *Wrath of Dragons* will have some dark moments, those dark roots are more Lovecraftian or *Doctor Who*-ish than *Game of Thrones*. It's not that I don't intend my series to shy away from adult themes, but it will probably land a bit more between YA and Adult in terms of the violence and thematic content. It's hard for me to write a book and not have humor in it and if I'm going to spend years creating and sharing a world I know I want it to be one that's a bit lighter with a sense of hope. Since *Wrath of Dragons* will have a lighter tone, its important I make that clear upfront. It's not that I can't include darker or more violent moments, it's that I should set the stage early so the reader knows what they are getting. I don't want anyone to pick up the book and think they are getting *Game of Thrones* because that's not the kind of story I am interested in telling.

ASSIGNMENT:

List at least three ways your novel will follow or twist reader expectations.

WRATH OF DRAGONS

ONE: Dragons - Mentioned above, my plan to bait and switch the animal-dragons for intelligent dragons.

TWO: Carter - It's very big in "book one" of an epic fantasy series for a character to unlock or discover magical abilities and get super powerful by the end of the book. Generally this happens with an orphan or farm-boy type of character. What I'd like to do with Carter is the opposite. I want to start the novel with Carter having power and have him lose his powers somewhere in the middle-ish of the novel. It will force him to see the world in a different way and be a great way to kick him to the ground.

THREE: The Big Bad - I don't want to have a traditional dark lord or Sauron in the book. I don't want a bad guy who wants to destroy the world or anything like that. I think I want to slightly hold back the plans of the "bad guys" and only reveal hints along the way so that there will be a certain point where the reader will ask, "who is the bad guy?" I want a bit more gray in the morality of my world than is seen in a lot of classic epic fantasy. In this sense, I think *Wrath of Dragons* will fit more with contemporary adult fantasies since so much of the stuff from the '80s and '90s were morally black-and-white.

ASSIGNMENT REMINDER:

List at least three ways your novel will follow or twist reader expectations.

LIST OF AWESOMENESS

ONE OF MY favorite assignments to give writers is to have them create a List of Awesomeness! It's a simple and fun thing to do, and at the same time, it can have a real impact in shaping the novel you are about to write.

To create a List of Awesomeness, all you have to do is write out all of the awesome stuff you want to put into your novel. The items on your list can be character, arcs, beats, twists, settings, themes, world building info, or just about anything else. There are no rules for making the list. Feel free to add anything that excites you about the story you want to tell.

To make your list, take two to three sessions, with breaks in the middle, and type without thinking too hard about it. Don't stress about making sure the list is perfect, because the list isn't a to-do list. This is a brain-storming session where you are listing out awesome stuff. When it comes time to actually structure out your novel, you will use this list as inspiration.

Because authors have unique voices, quirks in their writing, and different tastes, my list should look different from your list. If I list a lot of character stuff, don't think that you have to do the same. The only person who has an opinion that should matter in this is you. We already talked about reader expectations. This is the part where you set that aside and only worry about what excites you.

ASSIGNMENT:

Make a List of Awesomeness. It should be twenty to forty things things you wish to include or do in your novel. If your list ends up longer, that's alright, but try to make sure it does not end up shorter.

WRATH OF DRAGONS:

Here is my List of Awesomeness…

- Dark twisted scary creatures
- Mystery for the history of the world
- A magic system that is explained as the series grows and not upfront
- A made up language
- A strong theme… the idea that people can "make their own family"
- Dragons fighting
- Dragon poop

- Different cultures between the races and inside each race
- A hint at the mythology but not spelled out till later books
- Inside "easter eggs" that are glossed over but, upon finishing the book or the series, make so much more sense.
- A sense of fun
- A sense of bonding and growth between the characters
- A lone fighter taking out a dragon
- Different geographic regions of the world that feel different
- Different cities have different cultures
- Strong female characters who show its OK to be strong but still be vulnerable
- A blurry line between who the good guys and bad guys
- A big castle
- Lots of food descriptions of how it tastes
- A rogue Captain Jack/Han Solo character
- At least one or two sadder scenes that will make the reader really feel for the POV characters
- Strange non-earth creatures
- An in-world card or board game
- Bad guys who are later good guys and good guys that are later bad
- A sense that there is a much bigger world out there

- Show different types of magic hinting at multiple magic systems
- The reader makes an emotional connection with the characters
- A friendship with the older adult characters hinting at a past and history
- "Easter egg" references to Holiday Wars and The Zimmah Chronicles (my other series)
- A POV character that dies (to show that they can, and for other plot reasons)
- A world that has art, entertainment, and culture
- Working plumbing (so I can have baths and toilets)
- Magic technology advanced enough to match the printing press
- Lots of descriptions of how bad a fantasy world would smell
- An ending that is satisfying and wraps up this story, but sets up more
- A more hopeful ending

This is a weird list and going into it I thought it would be much more plot focused, but apparently the world building and underlying theme are more important to me than I realized. That's not too surprising because I'm already strong with structure. I'm not worried about the plot of my novel. What excites and makes me nervous is being able to create a world that can handle all the stories I want to tell in it and at the same time works and is believable to readers.

Your List of Awesomeness should look different. Unless

world building is your jam and important to your story, you do not have to have so much world building on yours. Focus instead on what excites you and what awesome stuff you want to shove into your novel!

ASSIGNMENT REMINDER:

Make a List of Awesomeness. It should be twenty to forty things you wish to include or do in your novel. If your list ends up longer, that's alright, but try to make sure it does not end up shorter.

It's now time to break apart your Story Pitch so that it fits into the basic three act structure. Don't worry yet about the novel beats. We will deal with those next. For now, your goal is to figure out the meat of what should happen in each act of your story.

My three Story Pitches for the POV characters of *Wrath of Dragons*:

CARTER: Carter, a magician's apprentice who often keeps his head too buried in books, desperately wants to be a hero and sees his chance to be one when he learns dragons are ravaging the kingdom. As the real world shocks some sense into him, he discovers his powers are not enough to stop the dragons. With the weight of thousands of lives hanging in the balance, he must find a way to save them and to do so he has to decide what matters more, being a hero or getting credit for being one.

DOUG: Decades after fleeing the dragon clans, Doug's kin return to the world of humans, killing thousands. In retaliation a "powerful mage" (Carter) accidentally turns Doug into a human and all Doug wants is to be a dragon again. Sucked into a world of magic, dark gods, and horrible creatures, Doug has to learn let go of his hermit ways or risk being stuck as a human for forever.

ALEX: Seeing her kingdom burn and her father unwilling to take action, Princess Alexandra Eos takes it upon herself to stop the onslaught of dragons. Upon discovering a dark mage is controlling the beast she has to lead a rag tag group of adventurers to find a lost magic. Should they not return in time, her father, everyone she loves, and her people will all die.

Having three main-POV characters means I have a bit of extra work. Instead of doing them all at once, I'm going to focus on Carter first. Pulling apart his Story Pitch it probably breaks down like this:

Act I: Carter, a magician's apprentice who often keeps his head too buried in books, desperately wants to be a hero and sees his chance to be one when he learns dragons are ravaging the kingdom.

Act II: As the real world shocks some sense into him, he discovers his powers are not enough to stop the dragons.

Act III: With the weight of thousands of lives hanging in the balance, he must find a way to save them and to do so he has to decide what matters more, being a hero or getting credit for being one.

My Act I is about setting up who Carter is, establishing a bit of world building so that the reader understands how things work, and then wrapping it all up with the reveal that dragons are tearing apart the kingdom. My Act II is the adventure. It's where Carter will head out into the world, get into a bit of trouble, and learn that his view of the world might not have been completely accurate. In Act III I'll have Carter learn from his ways, grow, and use that new knowledge to save the day. Carter's story is a straightforward character arc and the novel beats tied to him will conform to that.

If Carter were my only POV character I'd be sitting pretty at this point, but he's not. *Wrath of Dragons* is a beast, so let's break down Doug's Story Pitch into Acts:

ACT I : Decades after fleeing the dragon clans, Doug's kin return to the world of humans, killing thousands. In retaliation a "powerful mage" (Carter) accidentally turns Doug into a human and all Doug wants is to be a dragon again.

ACT II: Sucked into a world of magic, dark gods, and horrible creatures, Doug has to learn to let go of his hermit ways or risk being stuck as a human for forever.

ACT III: ????

I've discovered a problem. I failed in my Story Pitch earlier and didn't realize it. I made Doug's Big Want clear, but the core conflict wasn't. There is no clear reason why Doug can't turn back into a dragon again and it's not clear how his story ties into Alex's and Carter's. I know that I want Doug seeking a magic item and it's the exact same item that Carter and Alex need to free the dragons.

Seeing my mistake I can simply fix it here and keep moving forward, or rewrite my Story Pitch and then move forward. If I were writing this on my own without you watching, I'd probably just fix it now and move forward, but I want you to learn from my mistakes so here is his rewritten pitch:

DOUG: Decades after fleeing the dragon clans, Doug's kin return to the world of humans, killing thousands. In retaliation a "powerful mage" (Carter) accidentally turns Doug into a human and all Doug wants is to be a dragon again. Sucked into a world of magic, dark gods, and horrible creatures, Doug learns that the very thing that will return his dragonanity (humanity but for dragons?) is the same lost magic that will free the dragons from enslavement. Desperately wanting to be left alone and to return to his old hermit ways, Doug must choose between saving himself or the very kin that once betrayed him.

That should do it. Let's now break that into three acts again:

Act I: Decades after fleeing the dragon clans, Doug's kin return to the world of humans, killing thousands. In retaliation a "powerful mage" (Carter) accidentally turns Doug into a human and all Doug wants is to be a dragon again.

Act II: Sucked into a world of magic, dark gods, and horrible creatures, Doug learns that the very thing that will return his dragonanity (humanity but for dragons?) is the same lost magic that will free the dragons from enslavement.

Act III: Desperately wanting to be left alone and to return to his old hermit ways, Doug must choose between saving himself or the very kin that once betrayed him.

That works much better. Next up is Alex:

Act I: Seeing her kingdom burn and her father unwilling to take action, Princess Alexandra Eos takes it upon herself to stop the onslaught of dragons.

Act II: Upon discovering a dark mage is controlling the beast she has to lead a rag tag group of adventures to find a lost magic.

Act III: Should they not return in time, her father, everyone she loves, and her people will all die.

So let's combine all three characters into a single breakdown.

Act I

- Carter, a magician's apprentice who often keeps his head too buried in books, desperately wants to be a

hero and sees his chance to be one when he learns dragons are ravaging the kingdom.
- Seeing her kingdom burn and her father unwilling to take action, Princess Alexandra Eos takes it upon herself to stop the onslaught of dragons.
- Decades after fleeing the dragon clans, Doug's kin return to the world of humans, killing thousands. In retaliation a "powerful mage" (Carter) accidentally turns Doug into a human and all Doug wants is to be a dragon again.

Act II

- As the real world shocks some sense into Carter, he discovers his powers are not enough to stop the dragons.
- Upon discovering a dark mage is controlling the beast, Alex has to lead a rag tag group of adventurers to find a lost magic.
- Sucked into a world of magic, dark gods, and horrible creatures, Doug learns that the very thing that will return his dragonanity (humanity but for dragons?) is the same lost magic that will free the dragons from enslavement.

Act III

- With the weight of thousands of lives hanging in the balance, Carter must find a way to save them and to do so he has to decide what matters more, being a hero or getting credit for being one.

- Should they not return in time, Alex's father, everyone she loves, and her people will all die.
- Desperately wanting to be left alone and to return to his old hermit ways, Doug must choose between saving himself or the very kin that once betrayed him.

ASSIGNMENT:

Break your Story Pitch for your POV characters into the three act structure and then rewrite them to be a basic synopsis for your story. Don't let the synopsis get more than a page long and if there are any extra special twists, beats, or revelations that you know, feel free to include them.

WRATH OF DRAGONS:

I broke down my Story Pitches above, but here is the rewrite of my pitches into a basic synopsis:

Carter, an apprentice to Owen The Great, wants to be a hero, like the kind that appear in his favorite novels. Upon witnessing a dragon attacking, and Owen failing to take action, Carter confronts the dragon, only instead of destroying the beast he accidentally turns Doug (the dragon) into a human.

As powerful as Owen is, he can't help Doug so he sends Doug and Carter to the far off city of Compitum to speak with an Oracle. Along the way they meet Alex and learn that dragons are tearing up the kingdom to the south.

Upon reaching the oracle, Alex and Carter discover the secret to stopping the dragons is by finding a lost powerful flower called a "Dragon Lotus." Not only will the Dragon Lotus save the dragons, but it will also restore Doug to being one.

After side journeys and a bit of trouble thanks to a shape-shifting assassin, Doug, Carter, and Alex recover a single Dragon Lotus. Doug gives up the flower so that Alex can save her people, and it's up to Carter to use his magic and the flower to do so.

A massive battle with hundreds of dragons attack Alex's home city and castle. Our heroes arrive too late, and instead of "saving the day" they do their best to save who they can. Moments before the city is destroyed, Carter is powerless and instead of using his magic to free the dragons he is forced to rely on his wits.

That's the gist of what will happen in *Wrath of Dragons* and you can see how I expanded my Story Pitch breakdowns to reach those points. It's a good start and I can see enough of the overall story so that I can start picking out the individual novel beats.

ASSIGNMENT REMINDER:

Break your Story Pitch for your POV characters into the three act structure and then rewrite them to be a basic synopsis for your story. Don't let the synopsis get more than a page long and if there are any extra special twists, beats, or revelations that you know, feel free to include them.

SPOILER WARNING

FINAL SPOILER WARNING. The rest of this book contains massive spoilers for *WRATH OF DRAGONS*. If you have any desire to read *WRATH OF DRAGONS*, I recommend you read it first and then come back and finish this book. If you don't care about spoilers, keep reading…

NOVEL BEAT SHEET

BEATS ARE AMAZING. Screenplays live and die by structure and how they are used. You aren't writing a screenplay. You are writing a novel. That means that although beats are a good starting point, you don't need to follow them exactly. If you are writing your first novel and are new to writing, then sure, follow them until you get more words under your belt and better understand your voice. If you have one or two finished novels or half-finished novels, then don't restrict yourself and think that you have to follow the beats exactly.

Remember the beats break down of *Moana*? It used a straightforward structure and character arc. It's a Disney film, so that makes sense, but if we were to write the story as a novel instead of a screenplay we wouldn't have to follow the beats exactly.

The first act of *Moana* works great and it really does an amazing job of setting up the story and establishing the character of Moana, but the beats are on the nose. What if we kept the events of Act I but instead of them having in a chronological order, we wove them into Act II? Using the same story we could restructure *Moana* to be something like this:

Hook: Moana in a storm. She is sailing and failing at sailing. It's scary. We get a clear idea of how strong nature is and how powerful both the storm and sea are. Humans are powerless against both.

Meet the protagonist: Moana wakes to find Maui. She demands he come with her to restore the heart of Te Fiti. They instantly clash personality-wise and he ditches her. She uses her skill to catch up with him. We see how skilled and determined Moana is. We also see just how important this is to her, though we don't yet know why.

Status Quo: Moana and Maui are sailing, but she sucks at sailing and he lords that over her a bit. We learn here that her people were once wayfinders but lost the knowledge generations ago. We also learn that Moana left her people because bad stuff was happening and she is trying to fix it.

Catalyst: Evil coconuts attack. Maui and Moana call a truce so they can escape. They do.

Deal with Catalyst: Maui wants to know how a teenage girl even has the heart. This causes a full flashback or just deep POV thoughts of Moana's grandmother dying. On her deathbed Grandma gives Moana the heart.

The Big Picture: Maui agrees to get the heart, but only if they first get back his fish hook.

Moving into Act II we can weave in flashbacks of Moana and her father fighting. We can establish her character arc a bit more with her flaw being unable to find the balance of doing what she wants, wayfinding, with doing her job, being a leader.

Moana is a family-friendly film and so it has a short running time. If we turned it into a novel, we would easily be able to expand Act II. In the movie, only three main things happen in Act II:

- Moana finds Maui
- Moana and Maui find the fish hook
- Mona and Maui face Te Ka and get beaten.

What if the evil coconut things returned again, or Maui and Moana had to face off against more monsters, or they ran across other humans that tried to prevent them from completing their mission? Depending on the themes and the relationships you might be trying to build, you could do all of that and more here, while still revealing the stuff we skipped over by starting the novel with the movie's Act II.

When you are converting your basic synopsis into beats, make sure you think outside the box. Consider cutting information you want to hold for later, or telling the story in a non-chronological order. The beats make a fantastic start, but they don't need to be followed to a T and you need to make sure you let yourself as the author shine through in the storytelling. Sometimes that may even mean sticking to the beats.

ASSIGNMENT:

Adapt your basic synopsis to fit into a Beat Sheet.

WRATH OF DRAGONS:

With *Wrath of Dragons* I'm telling a big story. I have six POV characters. That's not unheard of in epic fantasy, but as an author it can be hard to balance and it can be off-putting to readers. By having such a large cast, it can create a barrier of entry that might cause non-advance fantasy readers to put down the book.

I want *Wrath of Dragons* to be the introduction to the world of Elderealm. If I were to break the entire series into beats, this book would probably cover everything from the initial hook to the catalyst. That means I want to take a few baby steps in this book. In the next book I can be a bit rougher and expect more out of my readers, but for now, I want the barrier of entry more on the lower side.

I'm choosing this not because it's "the right way to do it," but simply because it's how I want to do it. I could start off the book with the first six chapters told from a different point of view. It would be my way of saying, "If you can't handle this jumping around, then leave, because this book isn't for you." That is a valid choice to make as an author and that's the kind of choice you need to make for yourself and the story you are telling.

To ease the readers into my world, I'm going have Carter as the anchor of the story. He will be the first POV in the book and we won't cut away to another POV until Carter has met that character.

I'll also expand the space between my "Deal with the Catalyst" and "The Big Picture" and use that section of the book to really introduce the rest of the main cast. It will fluff up the length of my Act I, probably making Act I about a third of the book.

Hook - Open with Carter witnessing a dragon attack and going off alone to fight the dragon.

Meet the Protagonist - Carter confronts Doug the dragon. They butt heads and Carter uses magic to destroy Doug. The magic goes wrong and Doug is turned into a human.

The Status Quo - We learn Carter's home life situation and how he has been trained not just to be a magician, but also to be a healer. Doug on the other hand is having a hard time adapting to his new human body and learning human culture.

Catalyst Moment - Owen (Carter's Master) says he cannot turn Doug back into a dragon and that his only hope is to seek the help of an oracle in a far off city. Owen informs Carter that he must go with Doug since Carter created the whole situation and his magic may be the only kind that can undo the spell.

Deal with Catalyst - Carter and Doug travel to Compitum to see The Oracle. Along the way they befriend Alex, face a shape-shifting assassin (Kane), and learn that dragons are destroying the southern kingdom.

The Big Picture - The Oracle reveals that a dark mage is mind-controlling the dragons and the only way to save them is to seek a lost magical flower, called a Dragon Lotus. The very same flower can not only restore the minds of the dragons but also restore Doug's physical dragon body.

The New Status Quo - Doug abandons Carter and Alex to go his own way, while Carter and Alex decide to stick it out together.

Big Want Step 1 Attempt - Doug goes on his own by foot. Alex and Carter decide to take a ship and will sail to the island of Kale to get the Dragon Lotus.

Big Want Step 1 Fail or Success - Grekers (non-humans) kidnap Carter, Alex, Doug, and Kane (the shapeshifter assassin).

Status Quo Growth - Alex, Kane, Doug, and Carter are taken to The Greker's capital city and locked in a prison. It is revealed that Doug (the former dragon) is secretly the spiritual leader of The Grekers.

Big Want Step 2 Attempt - Doug will face challengers in an arena. If he wins, he and the others can leave. If he loses he will die, but Carter and Alex will be allowed to leave.

Big Want Step 2 Fail or Success - Doug defeats all the Grekers, but Kane then challenges him. She kicks his butt!

Status Quo Growth - Alex and Carter escape with an injured Doug on an underground river heading east.

Big Want Step 3 Attempt - Trying to get back to the surface, Alex, Carter and Doug face a dark monster.

Big Want Fail or Success 3 - Carter defeats the monster, but burns out his magic doing so.

Status Quo Growth - Magic-less (and keeping it secret) Carter, along with Doug and Alex, arrive in a shipping port. They need to hire a ship to take them to Kale.

Big Want Step 4 Attempt - They hire a sailor to take them to Kale.

Big Want Fail or Success 4 - On the way, a dragon army scorches the ship that the heroes are taking. The sailor is killed, but the heroes manage to make it to shore.

Status Quo Growth - Heroes swim ashore to Kale. The island is burned. The dragons scorched the entire island destroying all the Dragon Lotus.

Big Want Final Step - Heroes delve deep underground searching for any Lotus.

Rock Bottom - They are attacked by a parasitic monster. They fight it off and deep underground they find the Dragon Lotus. Kane is there waiting for them. She burns the flowers.

The flowers are destroyed and Doug has no way to be human again. The flowers are destroyed and Alex has no way to stop the dragons and save her people. The flowers are lost and Carter can no longer become a hero and when a fight breaks out he doesn't even have magic to help. As this happens a legion of the parasitic monster reveal themselves, attacking our heroes as well as Kane and the Grekers.

Epiphany Moment - While fighting the parasitic monsters Doug uses his bond with Kane and is able to defeat her. Doing so reveals a single Dragon Lotus. Doug decides not to use it himself and gives it to Alex.

Empowered - Fully as a team, Alex, Doug, and Carter work together to defeat the parasite monsters. They then team-up with their new strength and head back to stop the dragon army from destroying Alex's home city.

Climax - Massive battle. Dragons destroying the city. Flying. Fire. AWESOMENESS

Temptation Moment - Carter, who still has no magic, can't use the remains of the Dragon Lotus to free the dragons. He is forced to put aside what he defines as being a hero and trick the evil mage into freeing the dragons.

Epilogue - End scene of Carter, learning his magic isn't gone forever. Alex being a leader in front of her people and Doug adjusting to being half-dragon and half-man.

Keep in mind that as you do your beats not everything is set in stone and you don't need to know every single answer. The goal here is just to take your synopsis and flesh it out to the next stage.

Fitting your synopsis into the beats should be easy. The hardest part will be deciding what should happen in the middle. If stuck, ask yourself "What is stopping my POV character from achieving their Big Want?" Pick one to four major things that are getting in the way and create a Big-Want-Step-Cycle around those obstacles.

The idea is to leave this chapter with a skeleton of what your story will look like, something with a bit more depth than your basic synopsis and a bit more of you thrown into it.

ASSIGNMENT REMINDER:

Adapt your basic synopsis to fit into a Beat Sheet.

SEQUENCE OUTLINE

BEATS ARE USEFUL, but details of what happens between the beats is often missing. With a Sequence Outline our goal is to smooth out those beats so that they transition into each other.

For the sake of the next few chapters, consider a scene to be a part of the story with a set time and location. If a character is in the kitchen making dinner, that would be a single scene. However, if a character were to make dinner, and then they sit down in the dining room to eat it, that would be two scenes. This is overly simplistic and not fully accurate, but it makes outlining easier. Later, when I talk about adapting your outline and chapters, I'll talk more about what a scene really is.

A sequence is a group of related scenes. Those scenes can be connected thematically, through a setting, through action, or by some other means. The point is that the scenes are connected and when grouped together they form a sequence.

To help make it more clear what a sequence is, let's look at a few of the movies we talked about earlier, starting with *Wonder Woman*, which opens as follows:

- Young Diana watches the Amazons training how to fight.
- Diana flees her caretaker and is taken by her mother.
- Diana's mother and Antiope debate if Diana should be trained.
- Diana is tucked into bed and her mother tells her the history of the Amazons.
- Diana sneaks out and trains with Antiope.
- Diana is shown a sword that is implied to be a "god killer".
- Diana's mother catches a teenage Diana training to fight.
- Diana's mother agrees to let her train.
- Diana is training and uses her power to defend herself.
- Steve Trevor arrives on the island.

That takes us up to the catalyst moment in the movie. If I were to break those scenes into sequences, they would look like this:

Sequence 1

- Young Diana watches the Amazons training how to fight.

- Diana flees her caretaker and is taken by her mother.
- Diana's mother and Antiope debate if Diana should be trained.
- Diana is tucked into bed and her mother tells her the history of the Amazons.
- Diana sneaks out and trains with Antiope.

Sequence 2

- Diana is shown a sword that is implied to be a "god killer".
- Diana's mother catches a teenage Diana training to fight.
- Diana's mother agrees to let her train.
- Diana is training and uses her power to defend herself.

Steve Trevor crashing his plane would be the start of the third sequence. A clear overarching theme touches both Sequence 1 and Sequence 2, so the deciding factor I used in picking where to end the first sequence is that there is a time jump. The opening scenes are implied to take place on the same day. Once Diana sneaks out for the first time it starts a montage with Young Diana becoming Teenage Diana and then becoming Adult Diana.

Now let's look at the whole Act I of *The King's Speech*:

- Bertie is nervous and waiting to make a speech.

- Bertie stutters and messes up the speech.
- Bertie meets with a royal doctor.
- Bertie and his wife, Elizabeth, talk in private about his speech impediment.
- Elizabeth seeks out Lionel, a speech specialist.
- Lionel eats dinner with his family.
- Bertie spends time with his daughters.
- Elizabeth tells Bertie she found a new doctor.
- Lionel bombs an audition for a play.
- Bertie and Elizabeth visit Lionel.
- Bertie and Lionel meet one-on-one.
- Bertie tries to read a speech at home.
- Bertie listens to a recording of himself reading a speech and agrees to see Lionel.

If we broke these scenes into sequences they would break down as follows:

Sequence 1:

- Bertie is nervous and waiting to make a speech.
- Bertie stutters and messes up the speech.
- Bertie meets with a royal doctor.
- Bertie and his wife, Elizabeth, talk in private about his speech impediment.

Sequence 2:

- Elizabeth seeks out Lionel, a speech specialist.

- Lionel eats dinner with his family.
- Bertie spends time with his daughters.
- Elizabeth tells Bertie she found a new doctor.
- Lionel bombs an audition for a play.
- Bertie and Elizabeth visit Lionel.

Sequence 3:

- Bertie and Lionel meet one-on-one (it goes bad).
- Bertie tries to read a speech at home.
- Bertie listens to a recording of himself reading a speech.
- Bertie agrees to work with Lionel.

The sequences in *The King's Speech* break down easily with clear time, setting, or thematic cuts. The scenes fit well together and they feel like connected parts of a whole story, but keep in mind that this is working backwards. We are looking at two finished pieces of entertainment and deriving the structure from them. When it comes to creating your novel, we will be working the other way around, creating sequences and using those sequences to create a complete story.

When creating your Sequence Outline the cuts between scenes may not be as clear. You may struggle in knowing if a scene should be part of one sequence or another. That's alright. This isn't a make-it-or-break-it stage. If you envision a scene or two with one sequence but later in writing you realize they really belong to another sequence, your story will come out fine.

It's hard to prepare a list of sequences without getting distracted by the scenes that are in them. So as you move forward and prepare your own sequence outline, worry more about how one sequence will transition into another and about filling in any gaps. They main idea is to leave this assignment with a path that leads from the start of your story to the end with no breaks.

ASSIGNMENT:

Create a Sequence Outline for your novel. Be sure to personalize the sequences by giving them names.

WRATH OF DRAGONS:

Don't forget, *Wrath of Dragons* is epic fantasy. The novel will be over a hundred thousand words and so I will have more sequences and scenes in it than you most likely will in your novel. I'd expect your Sequence Outline to end up shorter than mine. Also, now is a great time to re-examine your List of Awesomeness and make sure that the things you want to include in your novel end up in one of the sequences!

Converting the Novel Beat Sheet for *Wrath of Dragons* into a Sequence Outline looks like this…

Dragon Attack! - A dragon attacks a small town and Carter, against Master Owen's wishes, decides to face it. Carter travels through the night and tracks down Doug, the dragon. They clash and the magic goes wrong, turning Doug into a human.

Human Life - Doug and Carter butt heads, but make a truce long enough to go see Master Owen. Owen informs them that to fix Doug they must travel to the far off city of Compitum. Before they leave, Doug starts to adapt to his new body and learn human culture.

New Friends - Doug and Carter leave Owen's cottage. Carter's big mouth gets them in trouble. There is a fight (maybe a food fight), with lots of witnesses (Alex and her Guardian see the fight). When the fight is over, Carter and Doug befriend Kate, a young woman trying to escape an abusive relationship.

The Caravan - Doug, Carter, and Kate board a caravan that will take them to the city of Compitum. On the caravan we learn a shapeshifter assassin is tracking Doug and Carter. Carter and Doug also meet Alex and Gideon who are also traveling to Compitum. (At this point the reader will know that Alex, Gideon, or Kate is the shapeshifter, but won't know which.)

The Red Hounds - A group of mercenaries attack the caravan. Alex, Gideon, Kate, Carter, and Doug flee into the woods. They meet Cooke, the leader of The Red Hounds and after a big battle Kate reveals herself to be the shapeshifter trying to kill Doug. Carter uses his magic to defeat Kane (Kate's real name) and our heroes flee into the woods again.

Secrets Revealed - Carter overspent his magic and is in a coma for days. In the meantime Alex and Gideon learn that Doug is a dragon and that Carter is Owen's ward, while Doug learns that Alex is a princess who went to see Owen requesting help in stopping dragon attacks. We learn more about Alex, the attacks, and the world and, after several days, Carter wakes up with his magic restored. We are told he has to be careful because magicians can burn themselves out.

Grekers - Gideon and Doug are captured by The Grekers, leaving Alex and Carter to save them. Carter shares an old story about how The Grekers worshiped one of the old races. With a bit of magic and trickery Carter and Alex scare off The Grekers.

The Oracle - Our heroes come face-to-face with The Oracle and learn that she is actually three women who speak cryptically and often finish each other's sentences. They reveal that Medrayt, a dark wizard, has enslaved the dragons and is forcing them to attack the southern kingdoms. The only way Alex can stop them is with the use of magic and a special flower called the Dragon Lotus. Doug learns that the same flower can return him to being a dragon. The heroes also discover that The Sisters (the Oracles) have manipulated their lives. Angered, Doug quits and decides to go alone. Carter agrees to stick with Alex and help her so he can be a hero and we learn Gideon used to work for The Sisters before he started working for Alex's father. Gideon says Alex's father must be warned so he leaves the group to go prepare for war.

The Big City - Doug struggles to leave the city. Culture and basic human needs thwart his way and he can't seem to achieve anything. Meanwhile, Alex and Carter visit her kingdom's embassy to make plans to get the Dragon Lotus, only they are attacked by Kane who had taken on the identity of the ambassador. A battle breaks out and it's so loud and big that Doug sees it. Swallowing his anger and pride, Doug decides to help. Just as Doug is about to have his butt handed to him by Kane, The Grekers return and kidnap everyone.

Secrets - The Grekers take Carter, Doug, Alex and Kane to their capital city. We learn a bit about The Grekers' Culture, and how they have a spiritual leader called the Arg'Natz. Kane, Carter, Doug, and Alex are locked in magic prison cell that they cannot escape. Kane reveals that Medryant, the one leading the dragon army, is Alex's uncle. It also comes out that Doug is the Arg'natz. That's why The Grekers captured him and Gideon and why they attacked again in Compitum. The Grekers want Doug to pass on the power of the Arg'Natz.

Arena - Doug agrees to fight in The Grekers' arena. He wins every fight. At the last moment, Kane challenges Doug. They fight, she wins. She gains the full power of the Arg'Natz and becomes the spiritual leader of The Grekers. In the chaos, Alex and Carter escape with a wounded Doug, stealing a boat.

Underground - Carter uses his medical knowledge to heal Doug. The three bond a bit, traveling on an underground river and the journey ends when they reach an ancient abandoned city. The city is infested with some sort of dark creature or creatures. Carter is forced to overspend his magic to help them escape.

Powerless - Carter wakes. He, Doug and Alex are on the great plains headed East. Carter discovers his magic powers are gone. He decides not to tell anyone and keeps it a secret.

Sails Ahead - Carter, Doug, and Alex arriving in a fishing port. They hire a sailor and head out to sea. While over the water they see an army of dragons. The dragons are headed toward Kale and they pause briefly to scorch and burn down the ship our heroes are on.

Kale - Alex, Carter, and Doug wash ashore at Kale. The island is burned to a crisp. It is why the dragons had been flying toward the island. Medrayt sent them to destroy all of the Dragon Lotus. Our heroes think they have failed. They fight. The Sisters (The Oracle) show up and say that deep underground some of the flowers were spared.

The Dragon Lotus - Alex, Carter, and Doug head underground and fight off creepy parasitic monsters. They reach a cavern and find Kane. She and an army of The Grekers are destroying the last of the Dragon Lotus. A fight breaks out. Alex, Carter, and Doug verses Kane and The Grekers.

Shoel - The fight awakens more of the parasitic monsters. Doug uses the creatures as a weapon to finally defeat Kane. Our heroes barely escape, but they manage to do so with a single Dragon Lotus blossom. Doug gives the blossom to Alex saying she should use it to save her people. Alex says she only needs a single blossom. She gives the rest of the flower back to Doug. He eats it and it turns him back into a dragon!

Dragon Fight - Flying, Doug carries Alex and Carter to Alex's home city. The place is nearly destroyed. They find Gideon dead and it's a full-out battle. Alex and Doug turn to Carter to use his magic and the Dragon Lotus petal to free the dragons. Carter admits his powers are gone and he can't! Alex and Doug tell Carter he can. They leave him to do his magic. While alone, Cooke (leader of The Red Hounds) appears. Carter tricks her into using magic to free the dragons.

Epilogue - There is a funeral for Gideon. Alex is nearly broken by his death. Carter is finally a hero, but still magic-less and Doug will either be back to fully being a dragon or maybe a were-dragon depending on the time of day (I've not decided yet).

ASSIGNMENT REMINDER:

Create a Sequence Outline for your novel. Be sure to personalize the sequences by giving them names.

SUBPLOTS

In Act II is the cycle of your POV character trying to achieve their Big Want. A subplot is any story thread that is unrelated to the POV character getting their goal. If handled right, a subplot can reveal character, create additional world-building, and add to the overall theme of a novel.

The bigger and longer your novel is the more room you'll have for a subplot. The shorter your novel the less likely you'll have room for a subplot. Let's look at Spider-Man's basic origin story. Not specifically one of the movies, just his general origin which goes something like this…

- Peter Parker is a nerd.
- Peter Parker is bitten by a radioactive spider.
- Peter gets superpowers.
- Peter learns how to use those powers.
- Peter uses those powers for personal gain.
- Peter sees a crime and doesn't act to stop it.

- The same person who commits the crime kills Peter's uncle.
- Peter decides to use his powers for the good of all.

The moment where Peter witnesses a crime and does nothing isn't a subplot because it moves the story forward. It's relevant because if Peter had gotten involved his uncle wouldn't have died, and if Peter's uncle hadn't died he wouldn't have come to accept that with great power comes great responsibility.

However let's pretend for a moment that the Spider-Man origin story was more like this…

- Peter Parker is a nerd.
- Peter Parker is bitten by a radioactive spider.
- Peter gets superpowers.
- Peter learns how to use those powers.
- Peter uses those powers for personal gain.
- Peter sees a criminal rob a bank and doesn't act to stop it.
- (Peter's uncle is NOT killed.)
- The bank robber uses the money to pay for his sick sister to have a surgery.
- Peter decides to continue using his power for his own gain and doesn't become Spider-Man.

The scene when the bank robber pays for his sister's surgery is a subplot. It's not part of the main story. It's extra story. That's why subplots can be tricky to handle. It's adding extra padding to a story. Too much extra stuff will hinder the feeling of progression and make a story feel like it's meandering and not going anywhere.

As tricky as they are to get right, subplots are useful. They can contrast or emphasize the theme of a story. In our Spider-Man example, who is worse: the bank robber who breaks the law to save a life, or Peter who is selfish and sneakily cheats to use his powers for personal gain? The two storylines contrast and make the reader see things differently.

Subplots don't have to be side stories with side characters either.

- Peter Parker is a nerd.
- Peter Parker likes Gwen Stacy, but is too shy to make a move.
- Peter Parker is bitten by a radioactive spider.
- Peter gets superpowers.
- Peter learns how to use those powers.
- Peter uses those powers for personal gain.
- Peter sees a crime and doesn't act to stop it.
- The same person who commits the crime kills Peter's uncle.
- Peter decides to use his powers for the good of all.
- With newfound confidence, Peter asks out Gwen Stacy.
- Peter and Gwen Stacy date.

In this scenario, Peter's relationship with Gwen Stacy is a subplot. It does not tie directly into the main story. It does serve the purpose of revealing Peter's growth that occurs over the course of the story. It's not uncommon that when dealing with a story that is more plot-heavy small character arcs will become subplots. If writing a story where the protagonist has a flat arc, but the supporting characters have arcs that don't tie directly into the main plot, those side arcs are subplots.

Let's look at another version of the Spider-Man origin…

- Peter Parker is a nerd.
- Peter Parker likes Gwen Stacy, but is too shy to make a move.
- Peter Parker is bitten by a radioactive spider.
- Peter gets superpowers.
- Peter learns how to use those powers.
- Peter uses those powers for personal gain.
- Peter sees a crime and doesn't act to stop it.
- The same person who commits the crime kills Peter's uncle.
- Peter decides to use his powers for the good of all.
- With newfound confidence, Peter asks out Gwen Stacy.
- Peter, as Spider-Man, disrupts The Green Goblin's plans.
- Peter and Gwen Stacy date.
- The Green Goblin figures out Peter's identity.
- The Green Goblin kidnaps Gwen Stacy to get revenge.
- Peter tries to save Gwen Stacy but fails to do so and she is killed.

- Peter takes down The Green Goblin.

In this longer version, what was once a subplot of Gwen and Peter dating has now become part of the main plot. Let's look at one more…

- Peter Parker is a nerd.
- Peter Parker likes Gwen Stacy, but is too shy to make a move.
- Peter Parker is bitten by a radioactive spider.
- Gwen's dad is over-protective and won't let her date Flash Thompson.
- Peter gets superpowers.
- Peter learns how to use those powers.
- Gwen's dad won't let her go out late at night to a party.
- Peter uses his powers for personal gain.
- Peter sees a crime and doesn't act to stop it.
- The same person who commits the crime kills Peter's uncle.
- Peter decides to use his powers for the good of all.
- With newfound confidence Peter asks out Gwen Stacy.
- Gwen says "yes" even though she knows her father will say "no."
- Peter, as Spider-Man, disrupts The Green Goblin's plans.
- Gwen stands up to her father saying she WILL date Peter.

- Peter and Gwen Stacy date.
- The Green Goblin figures out Peter's identity.
- The Green Goblin kidnaps Gwen Stacy to get revenge.
- Peter tries to save Gwen Stacy but fails to do so and she is killed.
- Peter takes down The Green Goblin.

The storyline between Gwen and her father is a subplot. If you compare this version to the last version the father-daughter relationship doesn't affect the plot in any kind of way. It is meaningful, though. It creates a small character arc for Gwen showing her becoming her own woman and not being controlled. It also thematically creates a bittersweetness because her dating Peter leads to her death.

You'll also notice that because this subplot creates a mini-arc for Gwen that, even though it is extra story, it doesn't hinder the overall sense of progression. That's the secret for making subplots work. They have to have a sense of progression.

When deciding if you are going to add subplots to your story, you have to ask yourself several questions…

- Does the subplot reveal character?
- Does the subplot add or contrast to the theme?
- Does it offer any other insight about the story, world, or characters to the reader?

If you answer "no" to all three of those questions then

consider not including the subplot or adjusting the subplot so that it does one of those things.

ASSIGNMENT:

Decide if there are any subplots that you will incorporate into your novel. Make sure any subplots you include reveal character, tie into theme, or offer some other important insight.

WRATH OF DRAGONS:

Wrath of Dragons is a mess when it comes to subplots, but that's because it's Book One in what I plan to be a nine-book series. That means even if a subplot may seem pointless it's really not because I'm trying to set up something that will come up down the road. That's a problem though, because as much as I'm trying to tell one grand story, I can't ignore the fact that *Wrath of Dragons* must stand alone.

The main subplots I plan to include in *Wrath of Dragons* are with my secondary point-of-view characters, Gideon, Kane, and Cooke. I'm giving each of them stand-alone scenes separate from the main story and main POV characters.

The way I've decided to deal with this is to make a small rule for myself. I'm not allowed to have any side stories in *Wrath of Dragons* unless they reveal character. This will mean that the subplots will be useful to the reader because it will add depth to the characters. It also means I can use them as misdirection.

The whole point of one subplot might be to set up a big twist that will happen two books later, but I don't want readers figuring the twist out yet. So if I make the subplots appear that they are only there to reveal character, then the readers may not figure out my real intentions.

This is not a method that will work for all stories or one that I think everyone should use. It's just a trick I'm hoping will cause a bit of misdirection and make the scenes feel meaningful without feeling like it's just set up for something that's coming later.

ASSIGNMENT REMINDER:

Decide if there are any subplots that you will incorporate into your novel. Make sure any subplots you include reveal character, tie into theme, or offer some other important insight.

SCENE LIST

THE WHOLE STRATEGY for outlining is to start big with your overall concept and then, bit by bit, narrow down the story by making choices that will reveal more details. Working this way allows you to deal with chunk-sized bits of story without feeling overwhelmed by them.

Now that you have a solid Sequence Outline, it's time to break each of those sequences down and to decide which scenes must take place in them. In addition to listing the scenes, you need to make sure you account for any subplots and make sure you incorporate items from your List of Awesomeness.

Remember, at this point we are considering a "scene" to be a set moment in time at a set location. For example, let's say you are writing more of a dark literary character piece. The novel opens with a car crash and the next scene introduces our protagonist attending the funeral of their father. While at the funeral, the setting shifts as the POV character flashes back to the last time they spoke to their father. Technically, the flashback is happening within the funeral scene and is a part of that, because that is the power of novel writing. To make things easier while creating your scene list, just count something like that as two scenes like this...

Goodbyes

- Car crash scene.
- POV character at the funeral scene.
- POV character fighting with their father scene.
- POV character leaving the funeral.

Later, when it comes time to adapt your outline, I'll talk about manipulating the boundaries of what is a scene and what isn't.

ASSIGNMENT:

Break down your Sequence Outline so that under each sequence you have a list of the scenes that must take place there.

WRATH OF DRAGONS:

Here is the first entry from my Sequence Outline for *Wrath of Dragons*:

Dragon Attack! - A dragon attacks a small town and Carter, against Master Owen's wishes, decides to face it. Carter travels through the night and tracks down Doug, the dragon. They clash and the magic goes wrong, turning Doug into a human.

All I have to do now is to look over the sequence and decide how many scenes it will take to get across the points I want to make.

Creating your scene list is similar to creating the original beats. When defining your beats, you were looking at the overall story and picking out which things must happen for the story to work. Now you are looking at a sequence and deciding what things must happen in that sequence for the sequence to work.

Here is the Scene List for *Wrath of Dragons*:

Dragon Attack!

- A Dragon attacks a small town. Carter and Owen see it.
- Carter tracks the dragon toward town, but it veers off course to the mountains.
- Carter decides to keep following the dragon. It leads him to Doug's cave.
- Carter confronts Doug. Carter accidentally turns Doug human.

Human Life

- Carter and Doug make a truce and go to seek Owen's help.

- Carter and Doug tell Owen what happened.
- Carter shows Owen and Doug the magic book he got the spell from. Owen tells them they have to leave in a few days. Carter and Owen fight about it.
- Doug explores the kitchen and experiences hunger.
- Doug finds Carter doing chores and they talk about Carter's fight with Owen.
- Doug and Owen have a late night chat talking about magic and the future. Doug and Carter say goodbye to Owen. Carter and Owen make up.

New Friends

- Doug and Carter get into a bar/food fight protecting a girl named Kate.
- Doug and Carter let Kate join them on their journey to Compitum.
- Doug, Carter, and Kate find their cabin on the Caravan.

The Caravan

- Kate's ex hires goons that attack Carter and Doug.
- Alex and Gideon save the day.
- Alex, Gideon, Carter, Doug, and Kate share a cabin to Compitum.
- A shapeshifter contacts the Big Bad. We learn the shapeshifter is pretending to be Alex, Gideon, or Kate.

The Red Hounds

- Mercenaries attack the Caravan and our heroes flee into the woods.
- Cooke (leader of The Red Hounds) says she is there for Doug.
- Heroes fight back and Kate is revealed to be a shapeshifter.
- Big fight, Carter unleashes badass magic and flies the heroes down a cliff to escape.

Secrets Revealed

- Alex, Doug, and Gideon almost fight, but call a truce. Secrets are revealed.
- Alex and Gideon talk about if Doug can be trusted.
- Carter wakes.

Grekers

- Carter tells a story about humans coming to Elderealm (the world).
- Gideon and Doug are captured by The Grekers.
- Alex and Carter track The Grekers.
- Carter uses his magic and tricks to scare away The Grekers.

The Oracle

- Doug, Carter, Gideon and Alex enter Compitum.
- The group confronts The Oracle and she is revealed to be three women.
- BIG info dump scene about the Dragon Lotus. It ends with Doug quitting the group and Gideon leaving to warn Alex's father.

The Big City

- Doug has hunger pains and struggles to get food. Ends up lost in the city.
- Alex gets in a fight with guards at her embassy who don't recognize her.
- Alex and Carter are attacked by Kane. (Doug intervenes.)
- The Grekers kidnap Alex, Carter, Doug, and Kane.

Secrets

- The drug The Grekers use on everyone doesn't work on Alex. She rides and learns a bit about The Grekers' culture.
- Trapped in cells, Alex learns that Medrayt is her uncle. Everyone also learns that Doug is the Arg'Natz.

- The Grekers challenge Doug to an arena battle. Winner gets to be the Arg'Natz.

Arena

- Doug defeats all of The Grekers.
- Kane challenges Doug and nearly kills him. She becomes the new Arg'Natz.
- Carter and Alex, with a wounded Doug, escape by stealing a boat.

Underground

- Carter saves Doug's life.
- Carter, Alex, and Doug bond.
- Group reaches ancient ruins and is attacked by dark monsters.
- Carter unleashes his magic to save their lives.

Powerless

- Carter awakes and sees they are on the plains. Discovers his magic is gone.
- Carter tries to make his magic work.
- Carter decides not to tell others he has no magic.

Sails Ahead

- Carter, Doug, and Alex hire a sailor.

- They set sail.
- They are attacked by a dragon army!

Kale

- Carter, Doug, and Alex wash ashore. The island is burned and there is no Dragon Lotus left.
- Carter, Doug, and Alex argue.
- The Sisters (The Oracle) arrive. Carter, Doug, and Alex argue even more, but learn a patch of Dragon Lotus was spared.

The Dragon Lotus

- Carter, Doug, and Alex are attacked by Shoel (parasite monsters).
- Carter, Doug, and Alex find Kane destroying the last of the Dragon Lotus. A fight breaks out.

Shoel

- Fight awakens more Shoel.
- Doug uses the Shoel as a weapon to defeat Kane.
- Doug, Carter, and Alex recover a single Lotus blossom.
- Doug and Alex split the blossom.

Dragon Fight

- Carter, Doug, and Alex fly to stop the dragon army, but arrive too late.
- They find Gideon dead.
- Massive battle with dragons!
- Carter admits to not having powers. Alex and Doug have faith he can re-awaken his magic.
- Carter can't get his magic to work, but tricks Cooke into freeing the dragons.

Epilogue

- Funeral scene with Gideon.
- Carter, still powerless, talking to Owen about everything that happened.
- Doug either being a human, were-dragon, or full dragon again (still haven't decided).

If you were reading carefully you'll notice that my scene list doesn't match my Sequence Outline 100%, though it is very close. That should be expected. The deeper you go into planning your novel the more it will evolve. The more you'll understand the characters and the more things will take shape differently from what you had originally planned.

I also don't have as much detail here as I did in my Sequence Outline. That's fine. Your main goal right now is just to figure out which scenes need to happen in each sequence.

When we do the full Scene Outline you will be merging and expanding this list with your Sequence Outline.

ASSIGNMENT REMINDER:

Break down your Sequence Outline so that under each sequence you have a list of the scenes that must take place there.

SCENE OUTLINE

IT IS time to make your outline! What you need to do now is take each of the scenes from your Scene List and figure out the elements that must happen in them. When done you will have an outline that will look something like this:

- **SCENE #:** 1
- **SCENE NAME:** Dragon Attack!
- **POV:** Carter.
- **SYNOPSIS:** A Dragon attacks a small town. Carter and Owen see it.
- **LOCATION:** Owen's cottage (on a lake).
- **STORY BEAT:** A dragon attacks, spurring Carter into action.
- **CHARACTER BEAT:** Carter decides to step up and try to stop the dragon.
- **OPENING:** A dragon is attacking!

- **POV'S IMMEDIATE WANT:** To stop the dragon & save lives.
- **POV'S LONG WANT:** Carter wants to be a hero.
- **INTERNAL CONFLICT:** Torn about Owen disapproving his actions.
- **EXTERNAL CONFLICT:** The dragon is attacking.
- **READER REACTION:** I want the reader to be like, "WTF!", and instant action.
- **ENDING:** Ends with Carter leaving Owen.
- **NOTES:** The dragon should be creepy and exciting, but the main conflict should happen between Carter and Owen.

An outline with so many parts could be a bit clunky in a word processor or in other writing software, so I've prepared a spreadsheet that you can use. If you'd like to snag the template, you can get it at the link below for free:

http://www.scottking.info/blog/outlining-template/

If you aren't a spreadsheet kind of person, don't feel like you have to use it. Outlines don't have a set form that they have to take. I personally am not a fan of spreadsheets and I didn't use one. I simply used a word processor and listed out my scenes like I did above.

When making your outline, create it in whatever way excites you. If you like mind mapping software use a mind map. If you prefer doing it by hand, then bust out legal paper or a moleskin journal!

Once you have decided how you want to construct your outline, these are all the elements that to include in it:

- **SCENE #:** This number refers to the order in which a scene will appear in your novel.
- **SCENE NAME:** This is a short-hand way that you will use to refer to, and remember, the scene.
- **POV:** This is the name of the point-of-view character for the scene. If you plan to have multiple POV characters for a single scene, then for now just list each of those incidents as separate scenes.
- **SYNOPSIS:** This is a brief synopsis of what you plan to have happen in the scene.
- **LOCATION:** This is where the scene will be set. When possible try to include any unique specifics about this location.
- **STORY BEAT:** This is the reasoning on how this scene moves your story forward.
- **CHARACTER BEAT:** This is the reasoning on how this scene either reveals character or moves forward a character arc.
- **OPENING:** How your scene will start.
- **POV'S IMMEDIATE WANT:** This is the thing they want right now in the scene. If they have multiple wants, list them.
- **POV'S LONG WANT:** For many scenes this will be your POV character's Big Want, but in earlier

scenes it might be something different or something tied to their character arc.

- **INTERNAL CONFLICT:** This is any internal conflict they are experiencing during the scene.
- **EXTERNAL CONFLICT:** This is any external conflict that they experience during the scene.
- **READER REACTION:** This is how you want readers to react to the scene.
- **ENDING:** This how you plan to end the scene.
- **NOTES:** Room for other notes to yourself.

This is a lot of information and you don't need to have all this information for every scene. For example, if you have a scene that is a major character moment, where the audience gets to know a POV character better, that scene may be all Character Beat related and might not have a Story Beat. So don't stress if you don't have answers for each of these elements in all of your scenes, but try to get as many as you can.

Conflict is one of those things that authors say "should" happen in every scene and I mostly agree with that but it just depends on the story. There might be a scene and the whole reason it exists is for a character reveal or pacing. Or maybe the conflict doesn't happen in the book. The conflict could be the reader knows a piece of information that the character is about to discover, which will cause angst and tension in the reader. If you are newer to writing novels, I suggest you try to make sure every scene on your Scene List has either external conflict or internal conflict.

ASSIGNMENT:

Convert your Scene List into a Scene Outline. Use whatever method (spreadsheet, mind map, list, etc.) works for you!

WRATH OF DRAGONS:

Below is the outline for the first twelve scenes of *Wrath of Dragons*. I'm not including the whole outline because it's too much info to share here, but enough happens in these twelve scenes that you should be able to see how I'm converting my Scene List into a Scene Outline by fleshing out the elements that occur in them.

I'm also asking my editor to NOT edit the Scene Outline. I want you all to see what I will actually use to write the book, typos, incomplete sentence and all…

- SCENE #: 1
- SCENE NAME: Dragon Attack
- POV: Carter.
- SYNOPSIS: A Dragon attacks a small town. Carter and Owen see it.
- LOCATION: Owen's cottage (on a lake).
- STORY BEAT: A dragon attacks, spurring Carter into action.
- CHARACTER BEAT: Carter decides to step up and try to stop the dragon.

- OPENING: A dragon is attacking!
- POV'S IMMEDIATE WANT: To stop the dragon & save lives.
- POV'S LONG WANT: Carter wants to be a hero.
- INTERNAL CONFLICT: Torn about Owen disapproving his actions.
- EXTERNAL CONFLICT: The dragon is attacking.
- READER REACTION: I want the reader to be like, "WTF!" and instant action.
- ENDING: Ends with Carter leaving Owen.
- NOTES: The dragon should be creepy and exciting, but the main conflict should happen between Carter and Owen

- SCENE #: 2
- SCENE NAME: Dragon Tracks
- POV: Carter
- SYNOPSIS: Carter tracks the dragon toward town, but it veers off course to the mountains. The dragon burns fields and the forest. Carter is forced to create a make-shift mask to breath through the smoke.
- LOCATION: Along a dirt road and sorghum fields.
- STORY BEAT: Carter is tracking the dragon, which will lead to a confrontation.
- CHARACTER BEAT: Carter is trying to be the

hero but lying to himself saying he just wants to help people.

- OPENING: A closer-view of the dragon. Last chapter we were a bit zoomed out but now we really get to see it.
- POV'S IMMEDIATE WANT: Wants to stop the dragon.
- POV'S LONG WANT: Wants to be a hero.
- INTERNAL CONFLICT: Feels guilty about going against Owen's wishes.
- EXTERNAL CONFLICT: The dragon is trying to kill people!
- READER REACTION: Reader should feel Carter is competent and be excited about Carter actually confronting the dragon.
- ENDING: Cater is given the choice to follow the dragon away from town or to go to town to help people. He chooses to keep following the dragon.
- NOTES:

- SCENE #: 3
- SCENE NAME: Talking Bullfrog
- POV: Kane
- SYNOPSIS: Kane watches as Carter scales a cliff and enter's Doug's cave. She is so bothered by this she uses a rock and is able to communicate long distance with Medrayt, her employer/partner.
- LOCATION: On a cliff outside Doug's cave.

- STORY BEAT: Introduce that someone wants Doug dead.
- CHARACTER BEAT: Introduce Kane and her not always getting along with Medrayt.
- OPENING: A shapeshifting/talking/magic frog assassin!
- POV'S IMMEDIATE WANT: Wants to kill Doug.
- POV'S LONG WANT: Wants to ruin The Sisters's (oracle's) plan.
- INTERNAL CONFLICT: Struggling with having to listen to Medrayt's orders.
- EXTERNAL CONFLICT: NONE.
- READER REACTION: They should be like "WTF?" and start to realize that there is a lot more going on than just a boy trying to kill a dragon.
- ENDING: Kane gets mad at Medrayt and hangs up on him.
- NOTES: "Kane' sounds too much like "Kate" and I don't want to give that away so only refer to her in this chapter as "the shapeshifter."

- SCENE #: 4
- SCENE NAME: Bad Magic
- POV: Carter
- SYNOPSIS: Carter confronts Doug. Carter accidentally turns Doug human.
- LOCATION: Doug's cave. (A dragon bathtub, crystal columns filled with biolumneseces).

- STORY BEAT: Carter's magic goes wrong and he turns Doug into a human (naked).
- CHARACTER BEAT: Carter uses magic he doesn't understand.
- OPENING: This is the confrontation we have been building towards!
- POV'S IMMEDIATE WANT: To destroy the dragon.
- POV'S LONG WANT: To be the hero.
- INTERNAL CONFLICT: None.
- EXTERNAL CONFLICT: Carter vs. The Dragon!
- READER REACTION: I want them to get to the end of the chapter and be like, "WHAT?" and at that point they should start to understand the tone and what kind of book this will be.
- ENDING: Instead of being killed, Doug is turned into a human!
- NOTES: This should be 1/2 scary and 1/2 funny.

- SCENE #: 5
- SCENE NAME: Bathtime
- POV: Carter
- SYNOPSIS: Carter wakes trapped in a pit (the dragon bathtub). He & Doug argue about what happened, but eventually make a truce and leave to go seek Owen's help.
- LOCATION: Dragon Bathtub.

- STORY BEAT: Carter and Doug team up for the first time.
- CHARACTER BEAT: Carter starts to come to the realization that he really screwed up.
- OPENING: Opens with Carter trapped in the dark and confused.
- POV'S IMMEDIATE WANT: Wants to escape.
- POV'S LONG WANT: To not get in trouble and be done with all of this.
- INTERNAL CONFLICT: Knows he screwed up and not only did he not save the day but he may have made things worse than they were before.
- EXTERNAL CONFLICT: Carter is stuck in a pit with no way out of it.
- READER REACTION:
- ENDING: Ends with them leaving to see Owen.
- NOTES: They should have a kind of buddy-cop movie relationship as the novel moves forward and for this part at least they should butt heads.

- SCENE #: 6
- SCENE NAME: Truthing!
- POV: Carter
- SYNOPSIS: Carter & Doug tell Owen what happened. Owen is PISSED.
- LOCATION: Owen's Cottage (Living room)
- STORY BEAT: Carter has to be honest about what happened.

- CHARACTER BEAT: Carter downplays how bad his choices were.
- OPENING: Owen is reading and annoyed when Carter & Doug (still naked) interrupt him.
- POV'S IMMEDIATE WANT: To get Owen to fix the whole mess.
- POV'S LONG WANT: To not get in trouble and be done with all of this.
- INTERNAL CONFLICT: He is upset and a bit shamed that his magic didn't work.
- EXTERNAL CONFLICT: He is being scolded and mocked by Owen.
- READER REACTION: Should start to feel sympathetic for Doug.
- ENDING: Carter reveals that he knows how to get into Owen's secret library!
- NOTES: Owen is mad. He is disappointed in Carter, but he also knows a bit about the future and what is coming. Part of his anger in this scene is him being mad at himself for not raising Carter better and because he is upset about having to let Carter go.

- SCENE #: 7
- SCENE NAME: The Library!
- POV: Carter
- SYNOPSIS: Carter shows Owen and Doug the magic book he got the spell from. Owen tells them

they have to leave in a few days. Carter and Owen
fight about it.

- LOCATION: Under Owen's cottage. Underground
  library hidden within the very lake itself.
- STORY BEAT: Carter shows reveals that he was
  able to use a bit of old magic and make it work.
- CHARACTER BEAT: None.
- OPENING: They enter the library.
- POV'S IMMEDIATE WANT: Carter wants to
  show off how he used old magic.
- POV'S LONG WANT: Wants Owen to fix things
  so he can be done with this whole mess.
- INTERNAL CONFLICT: None.
- EXTERNAL CONFLICT: Owen and Carter
  fight.
- READER REACTION: She be a bit awed at
  seeing additional magic and a more traditionally
  magic styled setting.
- ENDING: Ends with Carter and Owen having a
  big fight about what it means to be an adult.
  (OWEN says he can't fix Doug and that Carter
  must take Doug to Compitum to see The Oracle).
- NOTES: There should start to be references about
  dragons and the other Lost Races, starting with this
  chapter.

- SCENE #: 8
- SCENE NAME: HUNGRY!

- POV: Doug
- SYNOPSIS: Doug is hungry and he goes to the kitchen to look for food.
- LOCATION: Owen's kitchen.
- STORY BEAT: Doug is human and trying to cope with being human.
- CHARACTER BEAT: First time in Doug's POV. This is our first real chance to get to know him.
- OPENING: Doug explores a coldbox (?) or some sort of device thingy. Basically this world doesn't have electricity, but they do have some magic (agyl) powered technology. The coldbox-thing (needs better name) is basically a fridge.
- POV'S IMMEDIATE WANT: Wants food.
- POV'S LONG WANT: Wants to be a dragon again.
- INTERNAL CONFLICT: Doesn't understand humans or how to be one.
- EXTERNAL CONFLICT: None.
- READER REACTION: This should be a fun surprise, jumping into Doug's POV for the first time. Also should reallyyyyy start to feel more sympathetic to Doug.
- ENDING: Doug sees Carter outside and goes to speak with him.
- NOTES: After the last chapter, try to make it clear without being confusing that there are multiple kinds/levels of magic.

- SCENE #: 9
- SCENE NAME: Chores?
- POV: DOUG
- SYNOPSIS: Doug finds Carter doing chores. They talk about the fight Carter is having with Owen. Doug doesn't understand it or a lot of human stuff. Carter says he will try to teach Doug.
- LOCATION: Owen's cottage (outside near the lake)
- STORY BEAT: None.
- CHARACTER BEAT: More of Doug and Carter figuring out their relationship while the reader is still trying to figure out Doug.
- OPENING: Doug finds carer doing (blah chore).
- POV'S IMMEDIATE WANT: Doug want's food and to better understand how to be human (so it doesn't hinder his trip to see the Oracle)
- POV'S LONG WANT: Wants to be a dragon again.
- INTERNAL CONFLICT: Has no idea what he is supposed to say do or act.
- EXTERNAL CONFLICT: None.
- READER REACTION: A breather after all the heavier stuff that has come so far.
- ENDING: Ends with Carter agreeing to help Doug learn more "human stuff"
- NOTES: The chores should be something physical and medical related. (Maybe making bandages, or some sort of basic medical tool/supply)

- SCENE #: 10
- SCENE NAME: HashtagGoodbye
- POV: Doug
- SYNOPSIS: Doug and Owen have a late night chat talking about magic and the future. Owen asks some back story that the readers will have been wondering. At the same time he will say some weird stuff that won't make sense now, but will down the road. After they chat, Doug's words to Owen inspire Owen to make up with Carter.
- LOCATION: Owen's Cottage
- STORY BEAT: This is our "goodbye" to Owen. We won't see him again for a long long long time.
- CHARACTER BEAT: Our first real hint that Doug left the dragon clans a long time ago. Also he may not understand social queues but he seems to understand people and is able to give Owen advice.
- OPENING: Owen says goodbye and it goes from there.
- POV'S IMMEDIATE WANT: Wants to understand better and feel more comfortable with himself.
- POV'S LONG WANT: To be a dragon again.
- INTERNAL CONFLICT: Doesn't want to talk about his past even though Owen is brining it up.
- EXTERNAL CONFLICT: None.
- READER REACTION: Our final break before things will ramp back up again!
- ENDING: Carter and Owen make up.

- NOTES:

- SCENE #: 11
- SCENE NAME: Food Fight
- POV: Doug
- SYNOPSIS: Doug and Carter get into a local food joint (something like dumplings or ravioli). Doug has problems with social stuff, but does OK. Things get bad when Carter stands up to a thug/creep to protect a girl named Kate. Doug has to step in and save the day. In saving the day we learn that Doug has above normal human strength!
- LOCATION: A local restarturant (maybe attached to the Caravan depot?)
- STORY BEAT: Kate is introduced.
- CHARACTER BEAT: Doug has to actively decide to save Carter.
- OPENING: Doug nervous about his size, being human and trying to maneuver through a crowded restaurant floor.
- POV'S IMMEDIATE WANT: Wants to be left alone and then wants to save Carter.
- POV'S LONG WANT: Wants to be a dragon again.
- INTERNAL CONFLICT: Starts nervous and stressed about the surroundings and his size.
- EXTERNAL CONFLICT: Carter and bad-dude get in fight. There is magic. Carter gets blindsided and Doug steps in.

- READER REACTION: They should feel more sympathetic to Doug, annoyed with Carter, and then cheering for Doug!
- ENDING: Ends with Doug winning the fight after showing super strength.
- NOTES: ((The bad-guy is a hired guy working for Kane the shapeshifter. She is Kate the girl and this is all a setup. Also in the background Alex and Gideon are there to witness the whole thing.)

- SCENE #: 12
- SCENE NAME: Meet Kate
- POV: Doug
- SYNOPSIS: Doug and Carter let Kate join them on their journey to Compitum
- LOCATION: Restaurant back room.
- STORY BEAT: Kate officially joins the group.
- CHARACTER BEAT: After saving Carter, Doug is back to his grumpy I want to be left alone self.
- OPENING: After the food-fight (where Doug didn't get to eat) he finally gets to eat!
- POV'S IMMEDIATE WANT: Doesn't want Kate to come with them.
- POV'S LONG WANT: Wants to be a dragon again.
- INTERNAL CONFLICT: None.
- EXTERNAL CONFLICT: Between Carter & Doug disagreeing about if Kate can come.
- READER REACTION: I don't want the readers

to suspect Kate. I'm going to try and make her a bit cliche fantasy-woman. Also I want Kate to convince Doug that she should join and thus in doing so convince the audience.

- ENDING: Ends with Doug agreeing to let her join.
- NOTES:

ASSIGNMENT REMINDER:

Convert your Scene List into a Scene Outline. Use whatever method (spreadsheet, mind map, list, etc.) works for you!

A LOT HAS CHANGED since you first wrote an initial Story Pitch for your novel. The world, characters, and story should feel so much clearer now, and a good test is to go back and read your Story Pitch. Your finalized Scene Outline will either match your Story Pitch or it won't. If it matches you are good. Count your outline done and move on to Part III of this book.

If your outline doesn't match your Story Pitch you need to ask yourself why. What changed? Do you like that change more than your initial pitch or do you think your original Story Pitch is stronger? If your Scene Outline is better, then rewrite your Story Pitch so they match. If your Story Pitch feels stronger, you need to buckle down and make some hard choices about went wrong. Figure out why you like your Story Pitch better and adjust your outline so it rematches your Story Pitch.

Don't be scared of making a big change. Sometimes when pre-writing or writing you can choose the wrong POV character or go with stakes that are too weak. When realizing the flaws, make the changes you need to make, even if they are hard to write. Always go with the stronger choice. Now is when you want to mess up. Now is when you want to have to go back and re-do your outline because it's a hundred times easier to tweak an outline than it is to rewrite 50,000 to 100,000 words.

ASSIGNMENT:

Compare your Story Pitch to your Scene Outline. If they match you are done. If they don't match, decide which is stronger and restructure the other so that they match.

WRATH OF DRAGONS:

My Story Pitches and my Scene Outline match so I'm officially calling my Scene Outline done!

ASSIGNMENT REMINDER:

Compare your Story Pitch to your Scene Outline. If they match you are done. If they don't match, decide which is stronger and restructure the other so that they match.

ASSIGNMENT CHECKLIST

- Decide your POV characters and what kind of arc they will or won't have.
- Write a Story Pitch for your novel.
- Prepare for reader expectations.
- Make a List of Awesomeness.
- Write a basic synopsis of your novel.
- Fill out the Beat Sheet for your novel.
- Create a Sequence Outline.
- Decide upon any subplots that you wish to include.
- Break your Sequence Outline into a Scene List.
- Make the Scene Outline.
- Compare your Scene Outline to your Story Pitch.

PART III: ADAPTING YOUR OUTLINE

KNOW YOURSELF

THE SCENE OUTLINE you created is an amazing tool, but knowing how to use it is important. Your outline is not a finished product. It is not set in stone. It is something that will evolve as you create it and as you start to write. There are also a few other things we should cover before you head off to adapt your outline into a novel.

All writers have a unique voice. It sometimes takes a several books or a dozen books to find that voice and figure out who they are. If you don't know who you are yet as an author, I can't teach you how to do that in this book, but you can start your journey of figuring out by paying attention to your gut instincts when it comes to storytelling.

You are not me and I am not you. If you were to take the exact same outline I used for *Wrath of Dragons* and write a novel based on it, it would be drastically different from the novel I wrote. That's because we as authors have a different voice. We have different preferences when it comes to storytelling and what we like to see in our stories.

You might be an author who prefers a much slower-paced story or maybe you're more into character-study style stories than big arching plots. The outline you created with the help of this book can fit any type of story, but you need to know what you like and you need to listen to yourself to make it happen.

Your Scene Outline is malleable and, after going through the process of making it, if anything feels off don't hesitate to change it. Everyone has personal taste when it comes to a story. You need to rely on your taste. If you like reading novels with super-deep first-person points of view, then don't force yourself to write a third-person point of view that's shallow. If you don't enjoy humor don't add humor into your novel because you think you are supposed to or because you think the genre has to have it. If you hate happy endings, as long as you aren't writing romance you are probably fine having sad endings. Embrace your taste. Be who you are and make sure that your outline reflects that.

Once you get into writing and you are moving from scene to scene or from chapter to chapter, you need to continue to listen to your gut and personal taste. Your outline is an awesome road map, but if something more exciting or more special catches your attention, have the confidence in your ability to explore it. If it goes nowhere, you have your outline and can easily get back on track.

If your headspace gets too much into the "XYZ is supposed to happen" mentality, it will show. Your characters will make choices that don't fit and feel forced, or sometimes a beat that you thought you had planned out perfectly won't work. That just happens sometimes. It's not that you are a bad writer or that you failed at your outline, it's that the act of creating a novel is an ongoing evolution and you have to be willing to adapt.

ASSIGNMENT:

Really go over your outline and make sure it reflects your taste and who you want to be as a storyteller.

INCORPORATING THEME

ANY STORY you tell will have a theme. That's how theme works. It's a jerk like that, so it's always best to embrace the idea of theme and to make sure it's a theme you actually care about.

At this stage of outlining, you may not know for sure what themes will appear in your novel. Sometimes they don't reveal themselves till after you've done the first draft and that's alright. Just be aware that the choices you make now are already creating themes. If your novel has any kind of character arc, character with flaws, or an ending that is either happy or sad, then themes already exist in it. It may not be a big theme, but it is there.

If there is a story, there is also theme. What you need to decide is how you want to handle it. There is not a right answer or a wrong answer. There is only what works for you and your story. If you aren't big on theme and its not important to you, then let the theme be small, only showing through a subplot. If theme matters more to you, then let it be much larger and take up more space.

I'm big on theme and all the books I write have them. That's how I roll. I think stories have power. Stories creep into our heads and can change our perception or the ways we think. The stories we read when young, the ones we truly connect with, leave a lasting impression. If I'm going to devote my life to storytelling and those stories have a potential to influence others, it's a bit of a Spider-Man situation (with great power comes great responsibility). If I have this power, why wouldn't I use it? Not using theme and story in a meaningful way seems like a waste.

Last year I wrote a thriller called *Ameriguns*. It was in a way my response to gun violence that plagued the summer of 2016 with events like the Pulse Night Club shooting and the obscene number of police shooting victims. The strongest theme in the book is that if no action is made to make changes, nothing will change. The book doesn't offer an opinion on gun control, mental health, or how things should be fixed or changed.

I've gotten a bunch of hate mail regarding the book from gun advocates who say it promotes gun control. I've gotten an equal number of hate mail from gun control proponents who say it is anti-gun control. The best email I got was from a woman who survived a mass shooting that was a bit similar to one that happens in the book. It helped her deal and cope with what she went through.

I never expected that to happen. I never thought a real world shooting would mirror one from my book or that a survivor of a shooting would read it. Yet it happened and my booked helped.

That's the power of the stories. That's why when I plan and outline a book I make sure to make use of theme. It's a tool that we as authors have and I think it's a waste to not use it.

Not all stories have to touch a controversial issue. Not all themes have to be ones that could offer a person a new perspective of the events that have happened in their life. Sometimes the theme of your story may be as simple as "it's wrong to lie." All I ask is that you make incorporating a theme, even a simple one, a conscious choice.

Decide how you as an author want to handle theme. Will it be big? Will it be small? Wherever you land on the spectrum of theme, figure out what needs to happen to make that theme work in your novel. The more prominent you want the theme then the more the theme should show itself in the dialog, character arcs, or even the plot. The more subtle you want the theme, the less it should be touched upon and might only creep in via a bit of deep point-of-view prose or a subplot.

With *Wrath of Dragons*, my character arcs for Doug, Alex, and Carter are the most obvious places where the theme is clear. I knew going into this whole thing that I wanted each to have a traditional character arc. Alex learns a bit about being a leader and that she can't do everything herself. She learns to trust others and not micromanage. Carter has his world view of what a hero is shaken and flipped, while Doug, who has spent decades alone, learns again what it means to have friends and others you care about.

Beyond these things there are a lot of other themes in *Wrath of Dragons* and in the series as a whole. I've mentioned before that my big bad guy isn't really a big bad guy in the traditional sense. I want this world to be a more gray moral place. In later books, I want my heroes to have to make choices that, to other characters, will make them appear as bad guys. I want Elderealm to be a world where there isn't a perfect moral right side.

Wrath of Dragons is a massive book and there are a bunch of small themes that appear in it that will become bigger in later books, but the big themes in it are shown through Carter, Doug, and Alex's character arcs. The book is very much about characters growing, forming friendships, and creating a surrogate family.

ASSIGNMENT:

If there is a theme that is important for you to explore in your novel, make sure its threads appear in your outline. If you need to make notes, use the "additional notes" section of the Scene Outline.

CREATE YOUR CAST

WE HAVE TALKED VERY little about creating characters and I don't want to let you loose without addressing your supporting characters. On instinct, most writers will spend a lot of time planning, understanding, and getting to know their POV characters. That's good and that makes sense, but you should also devote time to figuring out who your supporting characters are.

Supporting characters are tricky because they only exist to serve the needs of the story. Supporting characters are placed into novels to reveal information, further the plot, further the character arcs, and things along those lines. Because they only exist to serve a purpose, it's easy for them to feel flat and fake.

Look at most mainstream action movies with a male lead or comedies with a male lead. If there is a love interest, that love interest is often one note and only appears in the movie to further the main character's story. Often this shafted role is assigned to a woman and it leads to women being portrayed as underdeveloped or flat characters.

Lisa, my wife, and I recently watched *Baby Driver*. It's a fun movie. It has great action and the structure and pacing are a bit different in a good way, but it has a serious problem with how it handles the character of Debora. Debora, portrayed by Lily James, is the love interest for the main character, Baby.

Over the course of the whole movie, all we learn about Debora is that she is pretty, she is a waitress, and that she wants to abandon her life and head west with no plans. Debora only exists in the movie as something that Baby wants and as Act II ends, something that he must protect from the big bad guy.

Baby Driver is a movie. It has a limited amount of things it can do in two hours. Novels don't work like that. In a novel, you as the author have the power and the time to flesh out your supporting characters. Instead of creating someone like Debora who is flat, forced, and weak, you have the room to create a character with depth.

To better understand what makes a supporting cast member tick, think about your own life. In your mind's eye, you see yourself as the main protagonist of your own story. You have a first-person view of the world and you have a bunch of wants and things that you desire in life. Every person you meet sees the world the same way. They are the star of their own story.

As I type this, I am sitting in Cafe Kolache, a cute little coffeeshop in a small mountain-ish town outside of Pittsburgh. My biggest want this week is to finish writing and rewriting

Outline Your Novel because I need to get it to my editor. If I don't get it to my editor, the book won't come out in time. If it doesn't come out in time I can't get it to my readers when I want to get it to them and I can't get to my voice actor when I need to. If I can't get it to my voice actor, I might have to find a different voice actor. Someone with a stupid name, like "Tom." I don't want anyone named Tom voicing my audiobooks, so it's very important to me that I get this book done this week.

Meanwhile, Lisa has a huge work project that is happening at her work. The whole reason we moved from the Houston area to the Pittsburgh area is because her company wanted her to oversee a huge project. Her biggest want and goal right now is to get that project completed.

Lisa and I often joke that with her job I am "support staff," like an uber-amazing personal assistant. Because she is so busy at work, I handle everything that is non-work related. I pack lunches, do all the cooking, do all the shopping, do all the cleaning, coordinate communications with family members for the holidays or special events, and all that kind of stuff. What's amazing is that from her point of view I look selfless. I look like I sacrifice my time so that she can do what she needs to do.

If we were to write a novel about Lisa doing her job and I were a supporting character in that novel, I would probably come off as a flat character. Showing that I had my own wants, like getting this book finished, would help add dimension to how I appeared in the story, but it wouldn't be enough. There needs to be more. Fictional-Scott would need to have a subplot or to have more of his personality revealed for it to work.

We could create conflict as Fictional-Scott struggles to get his book done, but still continues to do all the stuff around the house. We could even show Lisa offering to help out with some of the house stuff, but Scott refuses. Something like that would reveal that Scott isn't a selfless good guy, he's actually a jerk! It turns out that the only reason he does all the cooking is because Lisa is a meh-cook and the only reason he does the cleaning is because he's more of a neat freak!

This is obviously a ridiculous example, but you get the idea. Your supporting characters need to have lives of their own. They need to exist in your world outside of the scenes where they interact with your main cast.

In *Wrath of Dragons*, I have three main point-of-view characters and three small point-of-view characters. I did a decent job of fleshing out all six of them, but when it came time to do rewrites I realized I had another smaller character I did injustice to.

There are three or four chapters where the character of Tamaryn shows up. She's meant to be the sailor woman that takes Doug, Alex, and Carter to Kale. I knew going into *Wrath of Dragons* that I wanted a (*Doctor Who/Torchwood*) Captain Jack-inspired character. I wanted someone who was a bit fluid in their sexuality and a bit of a Han Solo-like rogue. Tamaryn filled that role, but beyond her personality I really didn't know anything about her.

When I got to the part of the story where I had to introduce Tamaryn, it went great. She's got so much personality and it contrasted right away with my main characters, but at the same time if felt off. It didn't make much sense why this character, who was a bit more on the selfish side and a bit of a con-person, would even do what the story needed to her to do. It made no sense that she would help out Alex, Doug, and Carter.

I had to take a break from writing and I planned out more of her back story. Once I better understood her and where she was coming from, I realized the only way she would help the main cast was if she was using them. I adjusted my outline and now those chapters with her are some of my favorite because, as they creep along, it slowly becomes clear that they aren't taking advantage of her— she's using them!

Your outline will keep you on track and keep your story headed in the right direction, but it won't breathe life into your supporting characters. So before you start writing, make the time to get to know them. Figure out the wants and needs of them. Figure out what things they do and what is happening in their lives when they aren't around your main characters.

ASSIGNMENT:

List out your main supporting cast members and figure out their wants and if they should have any subplots.

CHARACTERS KNOW BEST

You can have an amazing plot with tons of cool twists and surprises, but it will mean nothing if your readers aren't invested in your characters. There needs to be some sort of emotional resonance with your characters that your readers connect to. Without that, the story will fail.

Creating emotional resonance isn't easy. There aren't clear beats you can use to achieve it. It's something that you the author have to create through your own style and method of storytelling.

When I finished writing *Wrath of Dragons* it got sent to three alpha readers. I made tweaks. Then it went to a fourth alpha reader. I tweaked a few sections, but I also added additional chapters. The book then went to my editor. After that it was sent to nine beta readers in waves.

What fascinated me was seeing which readers connected with which characters in the story. One of my beta readers, the most geekiest and well-read with fantasy, loved Carter's guardian, Owen. The reader just wanted to know more and more about Owen and wanted Owen to have more "screen time".

Nearly all the beta readers hated Alex when she was first introduced. So many of them said she was "bossy," but by the end of the book Alex won over the readers. By revealing more and more of her and who she was as the story moved forward, the readers grew to care about her and eventually liked her.

A lot of the women who beta read were huge fans of Kane, the shapeshifter, and everyone loved Doug, the dragon who got turned into a human. I wasn't surprised that people loved Doug. From the start of *Wrath of Dragons* till the end, he is the most sympathetic character, but it surprised me how some readers completely gravitated to specific characters. There was no consensus with the beta readers. There were plenty of times when one reader would say something like, "Oh I loved Kane because she's mysterious, bad ass, and you can really feel her hatred toward herself and the other characters." Then I'd talk to someone else and they would say Kane was their least favorite for the exact same reasons.

Until you have people read your novel, you won't know what will click or not. You might have strong guesses. I kept making bad crap happen to Doug in *Wrath of Dragons* because I wanted him to be sympathetic. I didn't know it had worked until I spoke to a bunch of people who had read the book and I certainly didn't expect the readers to connect with characters like Owen or even Tamaryn.

No matter what you intend as an author or how skillfully you plan and try to manipulate your readers, everyone is different. Art is subjective and sometimes a reader will connect in a way that you never would have thought. Because there is such a wide variance in the personality of readers, the only way I've been able to truly create an emotional resonance between the reader and the characters is to create sincere characters.

Readers can sense bullshit. They know when a character acts out of character. If you want your characters to have that emotional resonance you need your characters to be genuine. The characters need to be fleshed out and they need to be honest to who they are. The only way you can make that happen on the page is by listening to your characters.

No matter what your outline says, always trust your characters first. Imagine you are deep in your novel and your outline says a character has to argue with another character. But now you know the character's voice and you realize that they would agree instead of arguing, so don't have them argue. Forcing a character to do something for the sake of plot destroys the emotional bond readers develop with the character.

Near the midpoint of *Wrath of Dragons*, Carter, Alex, Doug and Kane are held captive by The Grekers. Doug is the spiritual leader of The Grekers and they want him to fight in an arena so that they can take back the literal power that comes with being the spiritual leader. In my outline, I had Doug flat out agree to fight. It's what I needed to happen for the plot to move forward. When it came time to write the scene, instead of agreeing to fight, Doug said, "No."

It makes sense that Doug would respond in that way. Doug

spends most of the book wanting to be left alone. He wants nothing to do with Greeker politics and has no desire to fight people in an arena. So I had a choice to make. I could force Doug to fight, even though it was against who I had established his character to be, or I had to rejigger the story so that the plots and events forced him to change his mind.

I took the rest of the day off from writing, torn on what to do. I went for a walk. I spent all night thinking about it and the next morning I had a solution. Doug wouldn't agree to fight just to help The Grekers or to help himself. However he would agree to do it if it meant saving Alex and Carter. So I adjusted the plot saying that Doug would agree to fight in the arena as long as no matter who wins or loses it meant that The Grekers would free Alex and Carter.

I thought everything was great at that point. I had my problem solved. I was about to move forward with the sequence when Kane said, "Nope!" Kane is selfish and doesn't give a rat's ass about anyone else. She was not OK with Doug bartering for Alex and Carter's freedom but not hers, and she said that if they didn't work her into the deal she would kill Alex and Carter.

This created a whole new problem. I went for another walk at the park and I finally figured it out. I decided that Doug would legally adopt Alex and Carter, which would free them, even if he lost the fights in the arena. He would also marry Kane so that she would also be freed if he lost.

The whole thing is played as a bit of a joke. No one treats the adoptions or marriage as real because The Grekers aren't human. They have their own weird laws, culture, and society.

Doug treats the whole thing as nothing more than paperwork. That's when an idea struck me: What if it was more than paperwork and the characters didn't realize it until too late?

I wrote the scene of Doug and Kane getting married and, during it, The Grekers use a special magic that emotionally and mentally binds them together. The second the marriage happens, Doug can sense and feel Kane's emotions. She can do the same. The bond can only be broken by death, and it creates an amazing dynamic between the two for the rest of the novel.

When the arena fight happens, Doug and Kane face off, and based on the feedback from my beta readers, it's the best fight scene in the book. It was also the hardest fight to write. How do you write a fight when the two characters can sense what the other is thinking and about to do? It was a challenge, but it also added an extra level to the fight. It's also the first time in the novel that the reader starts to get a better understanding of who Kane is as a character.

When planning out *Wrath of Dragons* I had no idea that Doug and Kane would end up married. I didn't know they would be bound together by weird magic. It only happened because I listened to the characters.

As you write your novel and get to know your characters better, trust them. As easy as it might be to force a character to fit into a role that your outline says they must fill, it will come off false. Readers will see that and it will destroy the connections they have with those characters. Instead of fighting your characters, listen to them.

ASSIGNMENT:

Read through your outline, but don't focus on the plot and big story. Only look at the character wants and the beats that must happen in every scene. Try to anticipate any places where a character might be acting out of character and try to fix it now so that you don't have to fix it later when writing.

WORLD BUILDING

WORLD BUILDING IS one of those weird terms that a lot of writers think only applies to fantasy or science-fiction. It really doesn't. The act of world building is populating the world your characters exist in to create a sense of reality so that the readers think it might be real. Because of the nature of speculative fiction it is important that the world building happens when writing fantasy, sci-fi, and all of their sub-genres, but it is a tool that should be used in all storytelling.

World building is a con-game. It's setting up dressing and decorations so that it is easier for your readers to suspend their disbelief. Everyone knows that fiction is not real. Yet readers want to read a book and be able to forget that.

Picture a standard sit-com television set, something like the main living rooms on *Friends*, *The Big Bang Theory*, or *How I Met Your Mother*. The sets for these shows are created in a backlot building and are are only a half built. They have one full back wall and two half walls on the sides. The fake living rooms don't have ceilings because there needs to be room for the lighting rigs.

The sets are populated with furniture. Each piece of that furniture has been meticulously picked and placed. If you look closer, the shelves in the background will have books, magazines, trinkets, and sometimes call backs to old episodes. As random as those items might appear, they have been purposely placed to show a bit of character and to give the set a lived-in personalty and vibe.

There is an art director or set designer who is responsible for the overall look of the set, but they don't do the job alone. There are entire departments that support them. There is a props master and props department who goes to flea markets and pick up trinkets to acquire as props. Costume designers make, modify, or get the clothes that characters wear. The hair and makeup department ensures that the actors look like their characters. All of these roles and jobs have nothing to do with the plot. They are done for the sake of world building.

Your outline has the plot and character arcs of your story covered. World building is creating the set where that story will take place. It includes things like locations, the props or items that your characters will use, and the clothes they will wear, but it will also feed the back stories of your characters, show up in the prose descriptions, and even the dialog.

We already touched upon "write what you know," but let's go back to it because it ties directly into world building. Authors can only write using the information that they have in their head and build from the experience they have. When your story demands knowledge from outside your usual bubble, that is when world building is truly needed.

I've only shot a gun once in my life and I'm not big into guns. In planning to write *Ameriguns*, I had to learn so that readers who knew about such things wouldn't read my novel and be like, "…uhhh that's not how guns work." In preparing to write *Ameriguns*, I spoke to active and retired military. I talked to anti-gun advocates and pro-gun advocates. I watched tons of YouTube tutorials, read gun laws, and read about FBI procedures and rules. I also hired an editor who knew guns and was still serving in the military. These things are not the normal things writers associate with world building, but that's exactly what I was doing. I was gaining the knowledge I needed to be able to create the fictional world that *Ameriguns* took place in.

In *Wrath of Dragons*, Carter has a medical background. An ongoing theme in the book is that Carter can do more good by using his medical skills to help people than he can doing magic. I'm not a doctor and so I had to research to be able to write the few scenes where Carter shows his experience as a field medic.

When researching I like to Google first and get the basics. I don't rely on that information, I merely use it as a foundation so that I can talk to people with real-world experience and know the kinds of questions I need to ask. For *Wrath of Dragons* I spoke to two nurses and an ER doctor, all from different regions of the United States. I know that talking to real-world people can be intimidating, but sometimes it's the only way to get the information you need. The best part of reaching out to experts in any field is that a lot of times they are excited to talk about it. It's frustrating to be experienced in something and then to see that thing portrayed horribly in fiction, on TV, or in a movie.

I'm a big fan of the television show *Younger*, but I swear that damn show makes me roll my eyes all the time in regards to how it portrays the publishing industry. The show talks out of its butt. Every time they say something dumb or something that goes completely against how publishing works, I roll my eyes and am pulled out of the story. The bad world building shatters my suspension of disbelief.

Your life experience and the genre you are writing will determine how much world building you need to do before you are able to write your story. If you aren't sure about what you need to know, then I suggest starting with your main POV character and working outward from there.

Your protagonist is going to have different facets of their life. Start by building those. If I were to examine a character's work life in a field I knew nothing about, I'd start with questions like these:

- What does your character do for a job?
- What is their everyday work life like?
- What are their relationships with their co-workers?
- What kind of knowledge or skill set do they need to do their job?

- Is there a specific culture or lifestyle associated with the job?
- Are there any real-world rules, regulations, or laws you need to know about regarding how your character does their job?
- How does their job affect the other facets of their life?

Once you have enough world building done to understand one facet of your character's life, move on to the next. When that's done, look at your supporting characters and from there expand to what other knowledge you need to have to make sure your plot works and makes sense.

Unfortunately, I can't give you an exact set of rules on how much world building you need to do. You have to decide for yourself what information you need to be able to make the world of your novel feel real. The problem with world building and research is that you can get stuck. World building is a trap. I've seen it with other authors and I've seen it with students. I've had multiple students I've had to fail because, instead of getting their story written, they spent a whole semester working on nothing but world building.

For *Wrath of Dragons*, I spent a full month world building. I figured out a calendar system, months, days of the weeks, measurements, currencies for different kingdoms, history, and created a whole new language to use in the book. I love fiction and storytelling and so I worked out art, culture, and the different kinds of entertainment prominent in various regions. I grew up in two restaurants and so food was important to me, too. I figured out which crops grew in which regions, how that impacted the economy, trade, and developed recipes based on that.

It didn't end there either. After writing *Wrath of Dragons* I did a project I called *30 in Thirty*, where I wrote thirty short stories in thirty days. I used those stories to explore mythology and history of the world where *Wrath of Dragons* is set. It also let me flesh out the magic systems and explore characters using magic other than Carter and Owen. The things I discovered and figured out when writing those stories caused me to rewrite a few of the details in *Wrath of Dragons* as well as alter my plans for the later books.

I'm not advocating that all authors should spend two whole months world building. It's just what I needed to do and I knew it would pay off later. The majority of the stories I wrote for 30 in Thirty are going to be a spin-off series that I'll release in between the main books. The rest of the stories are actually going to be used in the main books. So it's not like the second month was wasted. Even though I was world building, I was still creating stories that could be released and sold.

Unless you are planning a huge second world fantasy series, you probably don't need to spend as much time as I did researching and world building. I went overboard, but in a controlled and planned manner. You need to look at your genre and the type of story you are creating and figure out what additional information you need to know to be able to tell it. If you are worried about falling into a research-hole, set a time limit. It doesn't need to be something as long as month.

It could be a weekend or an afternoon, but make sure you give yourself the time you need to get ready to write.

ASSIGNMENT:

Do whatever type of world building and research that you need to do to be able to write your novel.

CREATING MYSTERY

No matter the genre you are writing in, another tool you can use to keep your readers engaged is to include mysteries in your story. When done right, a well-placed mystery can grab attention and drive a reader forward to find answers. To be clear, I don't mean large overarching plots like where the POV character has to solve a murder or puzzle. I'm talking about small mysteries, the kind that can show up in a novel of any genre.

At its core, a mystery occurs when someone wants to have specific information and they don't have it. Remember the taco soup from my jacket pocket? The ultimate secret about the taco soup was that whenever I told someone I had taco soup in my jacket pocket, I actually did! As I'm sitting in the coffeeshop writing this chapter, I still have the soup. It's in my pocket. One day soon I'm going to take it out of my pocket but, for now, that is where it lives.

As you read this, a whole slew of questions might pop into your head…

- Does he really have taco soup in his jacket pocket?
- What is taco soup?
- Why would he have taco soup in his jacket pocket?
- Where did that taco soup come from?
- Why is this even relevant?

The taco soup is real. After gauging a person's reaction to me claiming to have it, I would reveal it. The reveal of the soup cut any kind of tension and there was always laughter.

Then, because I'm a jerk, I would put the soup away and pretend that I never brought it up. Of the thirty or so times that I did it, there wasn't a single time where the person wouldn't immediately ask why I had the soup in my pocket. It makes sense that they would want to know. When someone becomes interested in something, they want to know more. That's the power of mysteries.

Contemporary television dramas, especially genre shows, have embraced mysteries and it's a great place to see writers using them. Shows like *Westworld, Game of Thrones, Big Little Lies, Marvel's Runaways, The Handmaid's Tale, Better Call Saul, Stranger Things*, and plenty of others, are chocked full of mysteries. They leave the viewer wanting to know more, and that want and curiosity keeps the viewer glued to the screen.

The same technique can work in your novel and it doesn't require rearranging the plot, character arcs, or any heavy lifting.

If you had your POV character think about the "thing that happened in Venice," but don't upfront say what happened, that's the start of a mystery. Later you can have a second character refer to the same event, which will further fuel the reader's curiosity. Finally you let slip what happened. The payoff needs to be satisfying, but it doesn't have to be an earth shattering twist. Plus if you've layered out four or five small mysteries, wrapping up one will help further a sense of progress, which we all know is something that is super important for Act II.

A good ratio to understand is that the bigger a mystery is, the bigger the reveal and payoff have to be. When writing a mystery novel, the big mystery is the whole point of the novel and so the climax of the story is literally the big reveal and how it is wrapped up. The smaller your mysteries are, the less time you have to devote to the payoff.

If you create small mysteries in your novel, people will keep reading because they will want to find the answers. The easiest way to create a mystery is to withhold information. The people wanted to know why I had the taco soup because I didn't explain it.

In life, people can be stupid and they do stupid things. That's how the world works. But readers… readers are smart. They don't need to be spoon fed everything and when you are able to create mini-mysteries that pique their interest they will love you for it.

Holding back information can happen in all kinds of ways. A character might have a dark past or embarrassing event they don't want to share. The mystery may be about world building or the past relationships. The kind of mystery you create for the reader to solve will depend on your taste and the type of story you are trying to tell.

I filled *Wrath of Dragons* with a bunch of mysteries. The crazy thing is that the majority of those mysteries aren't for the characters to solve. They are there for the reader. I held back certain information and allowed the readers to figure things out for themselves.

One of the smallest mysteries in the novel is the word "unpoxed." It's a derogatory slang word. It's used a few times in the early half of the novel. The word is used in context, but not with enough information to make perfect sense. It's not until about two thirds of the way through the book before I allow a character to use "unpoxed" in such a way that the reader will finally figure out its meaning.

It's non-important information that I'm holding back. A reader can still understand the scenes and comprehend that "unpoxed" is an insult without fully knowing what the word means. I kind of threw it into the book for fun and it wasn't until I got into the beta reading until I realized how much people were grasping on to it. They kept wanting to know what it meant and when they were finally given enough information to figure it out themselves they felt like they had accomplished something.

Holding back information (details that the characters might know but that the readers don't) is a great way to weave in mystery. It's also hard to do since you know the answers. You want the mystery to be enough to make people curious, but not enough that they get frustrated. It's a thin line to walk and beta readers are amazing at helping you strike a balance.

I recently had two waves of beta readers for *Wrath of Dragons*. The whole point was to make sure that the mystery elements and the world building weren't too confusing. I had to make one or two minor adjustments based on word choice, but that was it. What surprised me most is that out of all the mysteries I had created intentionally and unintentionally, the readers most wanted to know about Carter's parentage and hoped that it would be revealed in Book Two of the series.

In *Wrath of Dragons* I establish that Carter was adopted and being cared for by Owen. There are a few lines or references concerning his parentage, but they were small because I had never intended it to be a big mystery. I had no idea that readers would grasp on to it as tightly as they did. I had always planned to reveal Carter's back story in a short story, but now I realize I can't. It needs to be a mystery that is resolved in the main series.

I'm so grateful to my beta readers. They have helped me fine tune and make the book better. I know for new writers that finding beta readers is hard, but if you decide to hold information back and use mysteries as tools to keep your readers engaged, seriously consider finding beta readers. No matter how well-planned your novel might be, sometimes you just don't know what will click with readers and you need to make sure that your payoffs are worth it.

Curiosity can make a reader keep turning pages and in real life it can make people do weird things. Humans hate not understanding something that piques their interest. If you ever doubt that, try putting taco soup in your jacket pocket, go out in public, and watch people's reaction as you tell them you have it.

ASSIGNMENT:

Consider what information you can hold back in your novel to create a small mystery that you will eventually resolve.

CHAPTERS

Movies, comics, television shows, and plays, are visual mediums. They are usually built from the ground up with scenes. Novels happen in the reader's mind and they don't use scenes in the exact same way. Because novels can go deep into a character's point of view, the border of what a scene is or isn't can become wishy washy. This is why, for the sake of outlining, I said to count a scene as events in a specific location and time. In reality, a scene in a novel could jump around in time or happen in multiple locations. So moving forward it can help to stop thinking about scenes and instead focus on chapters.

Novels are broken into chapters and there are no rules for what a chapter can be or can't be. You'll have to figure out on your own what you want a chapter to be, but before you do, make sure you understand that chapters are a tool for pacing. Chapters are a way for an author to manipulate the sense of time passing as a reader moves through a novel.

Thanks to the power of point of view, an entire chapter could take place between a single second of time. A chapter could open with a gun being fired, and then for ten pages be a character flashing back or reflecting upon their life. The same chapter might end with the bullet finally hitting the character.

A chapter might be part of a scene, a full scene, or a whole bunch of scenes. How long or short you want to make your chapters will depend on how you want to manipulate the pace of your story.

Short chapters will often make it feel like a story is moving fast and that the events are quickly happening. It's why you see so many thrillers with short chapters. The chapters might be one to three pages and there are no scene breaks in them. Instead of having a scene break they simply end the chapter because speeding through chapter numbers at a faster rate gives the reader the illusion that events in the story are happening faster. It's manipulative, subtle, and it actually works.

In epic fantasy, you'll often see long chapters running twenty to forty pages. It's because in epic fantasy, the reader wants to feel like they are getting massive chunks of story and really experiencing a different world. They want immersion and when they finish a chapter they want to feel like they got a meaningful amount of story. Fatter chapters does that for them.

When you convert your Scene Outline into a novel, you'll have to decide how many scenes you want to put into your chapter. When doing so, consider your genre but also consider the overall pacing of your story. Every kind of story should have moments that move fast and other that move slow. Even when writing a thriller there need to be scenes or chapters where the characters breathe and take a break from the action.

The breaks aren't there for the characters. Authors are jerks and don't care if their characters have a moment to think and reflect. Those breaks in the pace are there for the reader. Constantly ramping the action with no break will stress and wear out the reader. The reverse is problematic too. A story with no action and an utterly slow pace will bore a reader. To nail the pace between the fast stuff and slow stuff, you'll have to find a balance that works for you.

When writing *Ameriguns*, one of the things I liked to do was to structure a chapter as follows:

- Wrap up the cliff hanger from the last chapter.
- Give the characters (and readers) a moment to breathe and collect themselves.
- Ramp things up again.
- End the chapter with a cliff hanger.

The problem with this is that it's not always sustainable. If every chapter ends with a cliff hanger it will tire the reader and they will be more likely to stop reading in the middle of a chapter as opposed to at the end of a chapter. The way I decided to handle the cliff hangers was to use them within a sequence. When I got to the end of a sequence, I ended that chapter without a cliff hanger. Structuring my chapters in this way let me pull the reader forward, but not indefinitely. Ending a sequence with a breather meant they could put the book down and still felt like they got a meaningful amount of story.

That's what worked for me. This same approach may not work for you. Maybe it's too fast and you'd rather there were more breathing spots, or maybe you are anti-ending-your-chapters-on-cliff-hangers. These are the kind of choices you need to make about chapters before you start writing. You need to have an idea of how you want to handle them.

In *Wrath of Dragons* I didn't follow any specific rules for how chapters should be paced, but I did handle the chapters a bit more like short stories and didn't worry if a chapter ended up between 3,000 to 6,000 words. If things were too slow I did sometimes use a cliff hanger and in the next chapter I jumped to a different point of view, teasing the reader so that they would push ahead. I have a few chapters in the novel that are short, not even a page long. I have scenes that last a full chapter and I have chapters that are a bunch of scenes. I constantly varied the length of the chapters based upon how I wanted to toy with the pacing. My scene list for the novel had seventy-eight scenes, the finished novel has around ninety scenes, I think, and those ninety scenes are grouped into forty-seven chapters.

When you sit down to finally turn your outline into a novel, make sure you spend time thinking about the pacing and how and where you might went to start or end chapters. Never forget that chapters are just another tool for you to manipulate the reader and they don't have to conform to any kind of rules.

ASSIGNMENT:

Look at your outline and decide how you might want to break or group your scenes into chapters.

GO WRITE

As CREATORS, we have specific quirks and things that work for us. You have to figure out what level of outlining works for you. As long as you followed all of the assignments in this book, you should have a clear understanding of how to take a concept, how to apply structure to that concept, and how to keep adding nuggets of details till you have a full-blown outline.

I've taught students in a college setting and I've worked with writers outside of the classroom on a one-on-one level. Everyone writes differently and everyone has a certain level of detail that their outlines need. It might be that a full Scene Outline isn't for you, but a Sequence Outline works wonders or that you love the Scene Outline but prefer to jump right to it after creating a basic synopsis. If you've figured that out, that's amazing. My goal with *Outline Your Novel* has never been to say, "This is the one and only way to outline." My hope is that I could show you the whole process from start to finish and you would be able to take all or some of the tools and apply it to your own workflow.

From this point on, the responsibility to get your novel written lies with you. Writing isn't easy. It takes a sense of stubbornness. To start a novel, finish a draft, and then to start the rewrite process takes a commitment. Many people want to have written a novel but it's only a few who actually do it.

At this point you should have a fantastic outline and road map for writing your novel, but if you don't write it, it will never get written. Even if you hired a ghost writer to write your novel for you, it wouldn't be the same novel as the one you would have written. Only you can tell the story that's in your head the way that you see it.

Because writing is so hard, take the time to get your life in order. Adjust and manipulate your schedule in whatever ways you need to be able to make the time to write. If you can't find the time, it means writing your novel isn't a high enough priority yet in your life and if you don't make it one, it will never get written.

If you are struggling with workflow, or want a bit of guidance on prioritizing writing, check out my book *The 5 Day Novel*. If you have your ducks in a row and are ready to go, then go! Stop reading this or any other books about writing and go actually write your novel!

ASSIGNMENT:

Go write your novel!

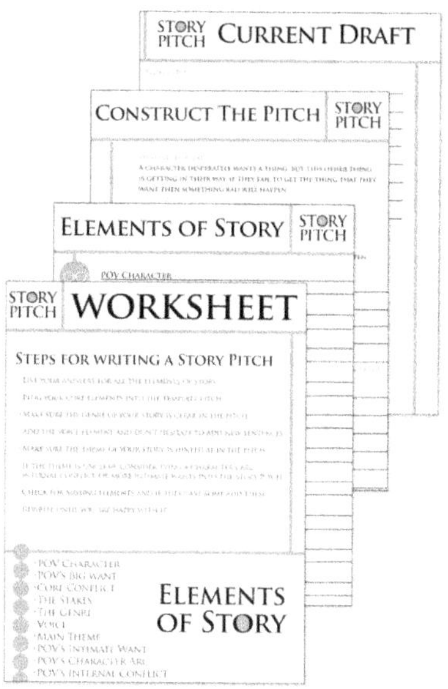

If you want to snag the worksheet for creating a Story Pitch you can get it here:

http://www.scottking.info/blog/story-pitch-worksheet/

If you want to get the spreadsheet template to use for a Scene Outline you can get it here:

http://www.scottking.info/blog/outlining-template/

Note to the Reader

Thank you for reading *Outline Your Novel*. If you enjoyed the book, I hope you'll consider leaving a review. They're the lifeblood of indie authors and the most important factor for other readers in deciding if they will pick it up.

ABOUT THE AUTHOR

Scott King is a writer, photographer, and educator. He was born in Washington, D.C. and raised in Ocean City, Maryland. He received his undergraduate degree in film from Towson University, and his M.F.A. in film from American University.

Until moving to follow his wife's career, King worked as a college professor, teaching photography, digital arts, and writing-related classes. He now works full time as a game photographer and author.

As a board game photographer, King shoots games for websites, online stores, and for other marketing needs. He also produces an annual calendar that highlights board and other hobby games.

To learn more about Scott and his work, visit his website at www.ScottKing.info. You can also follow him on Twitter via @ScottKing.